S0-BFX-267

RC
455.4
F3
F39
1987

The Family Therapy Collections

James C. Hansen, Series Editor

David Rosenthal, Volume Editor

Family
Stress

SCHOOL OF
CALIFORNIA
PROFESSIONAL
PSYCHOLOGY
LOS ANGELES

11/30/88 pub

AN ASPEN PUBLICATION
Aspen Publishers, Inc.
Rockville, Maryland
Royal Tunbridge Wells
1987

Library of Congress Cataloging-in-Publication Data

Family stress.

(The Family therapy collections, ISSN: 0735-9152 ; 22)
"An Aspen publication."
Includes bibliographies and Index.
1. Family—Mental health. 2. Stress (Psychology)
3. Sick—Family relationships. 4. Family psychotherapy.
I. Rosenthal, David, 1948-   . II. Series. [DNLM:
1. Family. 2. Stress, Psychological. W1 FA454N v.22/
WM 172 F1975]
RC455.4.F3F39   1987   155.9'24   87-11401
ISBN: 0-89443-622-8

Copyright © 1987 by Aspen Publishers, Inc.
All rights reserved.

The Family Therapy Collections series is indexed in Psychological
Abstracts and the PsycINFO database

Article reprints are available from University Microfilms International,
300 North Zeeb Road, Dept. A.R.S., Ann Arbor, MI 48106.

Aspen Publishers, Inc. grants permission for copies of articles in
this issue to be made for the personal or internal use, or for the personal
or internal use of specific clients registered with the Copyright Clear-
ance Center (CCC). This consent is given on the condition, however,
that the copier pay a $2.50 fee for copying beyond that permitted by
the U.S. Copyright Law. The $2.50 fee should be paid directly to
the CCC, 21 Congress St., Salem, Massachusetts 01970.
0-89443-622-8/87 $2.50

This consent does not extend to other kinds of copying, such as
copying for general distribution, for advertising or promotional pur-
poses, for creating new collective works, or for resale. For information, address Aspen Publishers, Inc.,
1600 Research Boulevard, Rockville, Maryland 20850.

Editorial Services: Ruth Bloom

Library of Congress Catalog Card Number: 87-11401
ISBN: 0-89443-622-8
ISSN: 0735-9152

Printed in the United States of America

1 2 3 4 5

To my mother and father
and all of my other
teachers

Table of Contents

v

Board of Editors

Editor

JAMES C. HANSEN
State University of New York at
  Buffalo
Buffalo, New York

JAMES F. ALEXANDER
University of Utah
Salt Lake City, Utah

CAROLYN L. ATTNEAVE
University of Washington
Seattle, Washington

JOHN ELDERKIN BELL
Stanford University
Palo Alto, California

EVAN IMBER-BLACK
University of Calgary
Calgary, Alberta, Canada

STEVE DESHAZER
Brief Family Therapy Center
Milwaukee, Wisconsin

HOLLIS A. EDWARDS
Toronto East General Hospital
Toronto Family Therapy Institute
Toronto, Ontario, Canada

NATHAN B. EPSTEIN
Brown University
Butler Hospital
Providence, Rhode Island

CRAIG A. EVERETT
Florida State University
Tallahassee, Florida

CELIA JAES FALICOV
University of California
Medical School
San Diego, California

DAVID A. FREEMAN
University of British Columbia
Vancouver, B.C., Canada

ALAN S. GURMAN
University of Wisconsin
Medical School
Madison, Wisconsin

PAULETTE MOORE HINES
Rutgers Medical School
New Brunswick, New Jersey

ALAN J. HOVESTADT
Western Michigan University
Kalamazoo, Michigan

Board of Editors
continued

JOHN HOWELLS
Institute of Family Psychiatry
Ipswich, England

DAVID KANTOR
Kantor Family Institute
Cambridge, Massachusetts

FLORENCE W. KASLOW
Kaslow Associates, P.A.
West Palm Beach, Florida

DAVID P. KNISKERN
University of Cincinnati
College of Medicine
Central Psychiatric Clinic
Cincinnati, Ohio

LUCIANO L'ABATE
Georgia State University
Atlanta, Georgia

JUDITH LANDAU-STANTON
University of Rochester
Medical Center
Rochester, New York

KITTY LAPERRIERE
Ackerman Institute for Family
  Therapy
Columbia University
School of Medicine
New York, New York

HOWARD A. LIDDLE
University of California at San
  Francisco
School of Medicine
San Francisco, California
  and
Family Institute of San Francisco
San Francisco, California

ARTHUR MANDELBAUM
The Menninger Foundation
Topeka, Kansas

BRAULIO MONTALVO
Philadelphia Child Guidance Clinic
Philadelphia, Pennsylvania

AUGUSTUS Y. NAPIER
The Family Workshop
Atlanta, Georgia

DAVID H. OLSON
University of Minnesota
St. Paul, Minnesota

VIRGINIA M. SATIR
ANTERRA, Inc.
Menlo Park, California

RICHARD C. SCHWARTZ
Institute of Juvenile Research
Chicago, Illinois

RODNEY J. SHAPIRO
Veterans Administration
Medical Center
San Francisco, California

JUDITH S. WALLERSTEIN
Center for the Family in Transition
Corte Madera, California

FROMA WALSH
University of Chicago
Chicago, Illinois

CARL A. WHITAKER
University of Wisconsin-Madison
Madison, Wisconsin

ROBERT HENLEY WOODY
University of Nebraska at Omaha
Omaha, Nebraska

Series Preface

The FAMILY THERAPY COLLECTIONS is a quarterly publication in which topics of current and specific interest to family therapists are presented. Each volume contains articles authored by practicing professionals, providing in-depth coverage of a single aspect of family therapy. This volume focuses on stress in the family.

There is an increasing awareness of the impact of stressful situations on the lives of family members. Families usually manage the normal stressful events in life; however, what is a normal stressful event depends on their perceptions of the situation and their resources to adapt. The family's structure, communication, and previous coping methods in dealing with stress affects their adaptive strategies. When a crisis first occurs a family will use their usual methods but feel overwhelmed when their previous pattern is inadequate. A family also needs different adaptation when dealing with   crises from living a chronic stressful situation. A family's methods that are effective in handling the crisis may become a dysfunctional pattern if continued over a longer period. When stress becomes a chronic condition, adaptation is an ongoing process and a family needs to adapt their perspectives as well as their behaviors.

This volume presents articles concentrating on chronic problems. Each author discusses the characteristics of a specific problem area and a model for treatment. The articles offer case illustrations for practical application.

David Rosenthal, PhD, is the volume editor. He is an Associate Professor in the College of Medicine and College of Education at the University of Iowa. He is Co-Director of the Marriage and Family Clinic and Co-Director of the Family Stress Clinic in the Department of Family Practice.

James C. Hansen
Series Editor

Preface

R esearch on stress and interest in examining the relationship between stress and a variety of life events has been extremely popular in the past few years (Goldberger & Breznitz, 1982). This interest has ranged from studying stress and employment, to examining stress and illness, to understanding the stress people feel living in a world faced with the threat of nuclear destruction. The initial focus of much of the early stress research utilized a disease model to explain causality, and disorders were seen as existing within the person. It is only recently, however, that researchers and practitioners have taken an interest in linking family with physical and mental health (Campbell, 1986). This approach or world view seeks to include an examination of the complex interactions that exist in any system, and understand the relationship between the external events called stressors and the impact they have on the organism of the family.

The stressors examined in *Family Stress* are indicative of our changing times. Fifteen years ago, families were not faced with decisions about transplantation or in-vitro fertilization. Only a few years ago, many people in our rural areas working the land believed they had found a utopian life free from many of the difficulties faced by those living in our cities. Furthermore, while our medical technology has advanced so that we are keeping people alive longer, we do not understand how the quality of that life will affect and be affected by those they live with.

In the first article, "The Stress of Infertility: Recommendations for Assessment and Intervention," Sadler and Syrop examine the impact infertility and its treatment has on families. They address the etiology of infertility and review various treatment approaches. The authors also review the psychological aspects of infertility treatment and present recommendations for marital therapists.

Logan Thompson describes the transplantation process through the experiences of the recipients and their families. The article summarizes the psychosocial aspects of organ transplantation and describes methods for treating families.

"Families and Chronic Illness" by Koch-Hattem uses case examples to depict the impact chronic illness can have on the family. With medical advances, Koch-Hattem suggests that more families are now faced with the increased possibility of living with a chronically ill member for longer periods of time. It appears clear that families living with chronically ill members are in need of support services.

In "Families and Chronic Pain," Hepworth argues that many family therapists are not adequately informed about physical illness and are concerned about getting involved. She provides the reader with a clear linkage between family dynamics and chronic pain, later suggesting more implications for treatment.

Nevergold in "Therapy with Families of Children with Sickle Cell Disease" points out the relationship between this inheritable disorder and family dynamics. She argues that in many cases, these families resemble those with chronic illness, and presents a case to illustrate the impact sickle cell disease has on the family.

The article examining post-traumatic stress and families by Rosenthal, Sadler, and Edwards suggests that there are a wide range of causative factors for post-traumatic stress. While the focus of previous research has been on veterans, one must remember that victims of rape, incest, and other violent acts are also at risk.

The last two articles move from medical stressors to environmental issues. In both of these cases, the situations are often a result of changing political conditions. In "Farm Families at Stress" Loeb and Dvorak make clear the concerns of farmers faced with the current crises in rural areas. These concerns are not limited, however, to those on the farm, and now extend to those working in farm-related industries and consequently their states of residence. In the last article, Fleuridas examines the stress of unemployment on individuals, their families, and communities. She calls attention to the need for an ecological approach, assessing the social condition that perpetuates family and individual difficulties, and working toward changing larger systems.

Each article in this volume examines specific stressors from a family perspective. The "patient" in each case should not be seen as the individual, but rather the context that individual lives in. The topic reviews and treatment strategies in each article should serve as guides, helping the practitioner develop strategies for working with these particular families.

REFERENCES

Campbell, T.L. (1986). Family's impact on health: Critical review. *Family Systems Medicine, 4* (2 and 3), 135–200.

Goldberger, L., & Breznitz, S. (1982). *Handbook of Stress*. New York: Free Press.

David Rosenthal
Volume Editor

1. The Stress of Infertility: Recommendations for Assessment and Intervention

Anne G. Sadler, RN, MS
Doctoral Student
Counselor Education
University of Iowa

Craig H. Syrop, MD
Assistant Professor, Obstetrics and Gynecology
Associate Director, In Vitro Fertilization Program
Division of Reproductive Endocrinology and Infertility
University of Iowa Hospitals and Clinics
Iowa City, Iowa

E pidemic numbers of couples today face the reality of infertility, defined as the failure to conceive after 1 year of intercourse without contraception. In the United States, one of six couples of childbearing age, approximately 18%, are infertile. The prevalence of infertility has increased over the last decade as a result of numerous factors, including the increased incidence of sexually transmitted diseases, work and environmental hazards, medication usage, and delayed childbearing. In a society in which most couples are concerned with birth control, too many health care professionals, legislators, and counselors perceive infertility as an unfortunate inconvenience and ignore its impact on the individual, the couple, and society.

All major religious groups and most members of society view procreation as necessary to the fulfillment of marriage. In addition, parenthood is associated with normal mental health (Rosenfeld & Mitchell, 1979). Therefore, childless couples are isolated from much of society by the unspoken stigma of infertility. The degree of stress and desperation felt by infertile couples is illustrated by researchers who found that couples without children are at a considerably higher risk of marital breakdown than are couples with children (Murphy, 1984) and that there are approximately twice as many suicides among couples that have been unable to have children (Seibel & Taymor, 1982). Family therapists must recognize that infertility is a major life stress for individuals and for couples. Competent therapy requires a basic knowledge of the infertility evaluation and treatment process and a clear perception of the stresses faced throughout this process.

1

ETIOLOGY OF INFERTILITY

As recently as 18 years ago, 40% to 50% of infertility cases were thought to be caused by emotional factors (Seibel & Taymor, 1982). Scientific advances have facilitated the identification of possible nonpsychological causes of infertility. El-Minawi, Abdel-Hadi, Ibraham, & Wahby (1978), for example, found pelvic pathology in 57% of patients with unexplained infertility. Current percentages of cases in which infertility can be attributed to a particular cause are 30% to 40%, tubal factors; 30% to 40%, male factor; 10% to 15%, cervical factors; 10%, anovulation; 5%, luteal phase defects; and 5% to 10%, unexplained or idiopathic factors. The combination of one or more of these factors in each partner may have a greater negative effect on fertility than any of the factors would have alone.

Female infertility has long been associated with "deep-seated personality maladjustment" (Brand, 1982). Several researchers have characterized infertile women as more neurotic, dependent, and anxious than are fertile women, suggesting that infertile women experience fear associated with reproduction and conflict over their femininity (Seibel & Taymor, 1982). Conversely, others have described infertile women as more outgoing, warmhearted, and even-tempered than are fertile women (Klemer, Rutherford, Banks, & Coburn, 1966).

Some researchers have speculated that infertility may be part of a coping system for women. For example, some women may develop rigid ego defenses against their biological needs as a means of incorporating current career-oriented value systems (Benedek, 1952; Denber, 1978), or the inability to conceive may be a way to accommodate the culturally approved desire for pregnancy without guilt for enjoying work and escaping motherhood (Allison, 1979; McCartney, 1985).

Infertility literature rarely focuses on the psychological aspects of male infertility. Sexual disturbances, such as infrequent coitus and performance disorders, are most frequently investigated. After reviewing 18 such studies, Bents (1985) concluded that sexual disturbances may diminish, but do not eradicate, the chance of conception. Moreover, in a review of 53 articles on the psychology of male infertility, Bents found no specific emotional factors that have a significant influence on infertility.

It is generally believed that pregnancy will follow the resolution of psychological conflict. The literature, however, does not support this assumption. Noyes and Chapnick (1964), citing 75 references with approximately 50 psychological correlates to fertility problems, concluded that there is no evidence to prove that any specific psychological factor can alter fertility in the "normal infertile couple." Also widespread is the impression that an infertile couple that adopts a child will subsequently achieve pregnancy. Although this does occur in a small percentage of cases, studies indicate overwhelmingly that there is no relationship between adoption and subsequent conception (Aronson & Glienke, 1963; Banks, 1965; Cooper, 1971; Seibel & Taymor, 1982; Tyler, 1960).

In summary, few studies show that psychological problems preceded the infertility rather than resulted from it. There is no literature to support the hypothesis that specific emotional factors or unresolved psychological conflicts have a significant impact on infertility. The common acceptance of these erroneous views may result in inadequate and sometimes inhumane patient treatment.

RECOGNITION OF INFERTILITY AND DESIRE FOR TREATMENT

It is estimated that 75% of couples that suspect infertility seek treatment (Amelar, Dublen, & Walsh, 1977). Seeking infertility treatment is a couple's first active attempt to come to terms with their infertility. In most cases, the woman is first to recognize infertility as a problem, initiate open discussion on the subject, and arrange the first medical contact (Lalos, Lalos, Jacobsson, & von Schoultz, 1985). Most patients wait longer than the established 1-year time period before they seek treatment. They may be fearful of a negative diagnosis, anxious to avoid the emotional stress and physical pain of the investigation and diagnosis, and reluctant to give up control of their own efforts to conceive (Lalos et al., 1985). Some have speculated that the infertile fear harm, castration, or mutilation of their reproductive organs (Griffin, 1983).

Not all couples that seek infertility treatment want to be parents. Infertility can be a symptom of unresolved conflict or stressors that the couple cannot satisfactorily resolve alone. Motives for infertility treatment include

- pressures from extended family
- marital discord
- replacement of loss (e.g., prior abortion, loss of career, significant death)
- desire for a career alternative or replacement
- desire to be "healthy and complete"
- attainment of adulthood
- displacement of stepchildren and establishment of permanence/dominance of new marriage
- resolution of sexual dysfunction
- reaction to change in family roles or power (e.g., husband graduates, wife returns to work and makes more money than husband does)

- fear of infertility secondary to knowledge acquired from the media or from family or friends who are infertile
- attempts to follow life cycle

It is imperative for couples to contemplate whether seeking infertility treatment reflects a desire for generativity or is a symptom of some other problem that requires different therapeutic approaches. Pregnancy is not always the ultimate resolution of infertility.

Couples must also examine their individual and mutual fertility goals. One partner sometimes assumes that the other has the same goals when, in reality, the other does not want to have children at the present time, but will "go along with treatment." Couples may explain their infertility by means of "myths" that may seem to be unrealistic, but are nonetheless disturbing and create distance. Patient education is invaluable in addressing such misconceptions, as well as in explaining the procedures involved in an infertility assessment.

By the time of the initial appointment, couples have already progressed to some phase of "the crisis of infertility." This emotional state includes feelings of surprise, denial, anger, isolation, and grief, generally in that order (Menning, 1979); however, couples generally hide these feelings from unfamiliar infertility specialists. Despite any delay in seeking treatment, patients are anxious for a diagnosis and prediction of fertility during the initial office visit. They desperately seek information about what to expect throughout treatment and a firm plan of action.

INFERTILITY EVALUATION

Not every couple that seeks an infertility evaluation requires an intensive or invasive investigation. Basic education, reassurance, and guidance are major parts of the treatment and may be sufficient.

Medical Aspects of an Infertility Evaluation

The initial visit to a reproductive endocrinologist commonly includes:

- a detailed interview, including a discussion of the woman's gynecological and developmental history
- a sexual history, detailing coital frequency, prior contraceptive use, and exposure to sexually transmitted diseases
- a past medical history and a complete physical examination

- blood testing of ovarian and/or pituitary hormones, depending on the presence of any problems and the phase of the menstrual cycle
- scheduling or performance of a complete analysis of the man's semen, with referral to an andrologist should an abnormality be discovered

Additional studies are designed to identify specific infertility factors. For example, the following diagnostic procedures are performed to determine whether infertility is attributable to the male factor:

1. semen analysis, single or serial. If findings are abnormal, the patient is referred to an andrologist, who may require scrotal ultrasound (Doppler) examinations, spermatic vein venograms, or determination of peripheral blood hormone levels.
2. examination for the presence of autosperm antibodies of semenal fluid or serum, commonly performed when infertility is unexplained or postcoital findings are abnormal.
3. sperm penetration assay ("hamster test"), usually performed when infertility is unexplained or findings of the semen analysis are abnormal.

Several female factors are also investigated:

1. ovulatory.

   - Basal body temperatures imply ovulation and luteal phase length. Preovulatory urinary testing for luteinizing hormone provides a more accurate indication of ovulation and helps to determine the proper timing of coitus or insemination. Pelvic ultrasound examinations document follicle growth and collapse, implying ovulation.
   - Determinations of serum progesterone levels and/or endometrial biopsies are used to assess postovulatory ovarian function, the presence of ovulatory dysfunction, or luteal phase defects.

2. cervical/mucus. Postcoital examinations (Sims-Huhner tests) explore mucus-sperm interactions. Results sometimes indicate the need for antisperm antibody testing. Scant or abnormal cervical mucus may require therapy to improve mucus quality.
3. uterotubal.

   - Hysterosalpingogram (contrast dye insufflation of the uterus and fallopian tubes followed by radiologic examination) screens for tubal patency and the presence of uterine cavity abnormalities.

- Diagnostic laparoscopy and hysteroscopy are invasive procedures to investigate and/or treat tubal or uterine disease.

4. intraperitoneal factors. Diagnostic laparoscopy may be used to document the presence of endometriosis or peritubal/periovarian adhesions.

Psychological Aspects of an Infertility Evaluation

Many initial appointments for an infertility evaluation do not end with the identification of a specific problem(s) as the reason for infertility. Because the medical evaluation of infertility is intensive and sometimes lengthy, patients must endure the physical discomfort and hassles associated with repeated appointments. The psychological aspects of the evaluation create additional strain for the infertile. In a pretreatment investigation of 200 couples, 49% of the women and 15% of the men described infertility as their most upsetting life experience.

A person's identity is shaped around feelings about body image, physical well-being, and perceptions of physical endurance, intactness, or defectiveness (Kraft et al., 1980). Infertility assessments often reveal a medical problem in a "healthy" person, however. Although the problem usually has no outward physical manifestations, the patient must form a new self-image. Feelings of betrayal, guilt, and failure, together with fear of abandonment, are common. Identification as the partner with the infertility problem can be particularly stressful, especially if this individual is the dominant partner in the family hierarchy. Follow-up appointments may further isolate the identified patient from the family system and contribute to additional discomfort. The partner not involved in investigative follow-up (often the male) feels excluded from the process.

The cause of infertility may influence the patient's perception of both self and spouse. Keye, Deneris, Butell, Wilson, and Sullivan (1983) evaluated the effect on women of various causes of infertility and found that women with ovulatory dysfunction felt inadequate, had a poor body image, and had low self-esteem. Patients with tubal disease often felt guilty and punished. Patients with endometriosis described themselves as feeling helpless. Women whose husbands had a male factor were dissatisfied with sex. Berger (1980) also noted that wives in couples with male factor infertility reported sexual dissatisfaction, as well as alternate rage and protectiveness toward their husbands. These wives frequently had dreams in which the husband was violently injured or died, and they experienced guilt and sadness about their feelings. Husbands (80%) were often impotent for 3 weeks after diagnosis.

INFERTILITY TREATMENT

Medical Aspects of Infertility Treatment

The treatment selected and the probability of its success are highly dependent on the infertility factor(s) identified. Male factor interventions may involve medications (e.g., clomiphene citrate, gonadotropins) or surgical therapy (e.g., varicocele repair), special laboratory preparations (e.g., intrauterine insemination, artificial insemination of husband or donor sperm) to overcome deficient semen parameters. Likewise, many factors that affect female fertility are amenable to medication, surgery, or a combination of the two. Ovulatory dysfunction is usually responsive to medications (e.g., bromocriptine, clomiphene citrate, gonadotropins, or gonadotropin-releasing hormone) but rarely does, of itself, require surgery. Abnormal cervical mucus is often treated by medications (e.g., estrogens, antibiotics, gonadotropins). Endometriosis, a major peritoneal cavity factor in infertility, is managed by medications (e.g., danazol, progestins, gonadotropin-releasing hormone analogs) or surgery—singly, sequentially, or jointly. Tubal or adhesive disease may be surgically corrected in some cases.

Infertility therapy may require prolonged periods of treatment and follow-up, amounting to months or years. Those who treat the infertile couple serve as the agents who announce to the couple their stage in this passage through treatment as well as the likely destination of treatment (Matthews & Matthews, 1986). Approximately 50% of couples with an identified organic cause of infertility achieve pregnancy.

Psychological Aspects of Infertility Treatment

Those who commit themselves to infertility treatment find their life styles radically altered by numerous appointments, ovulatory charts, painful procedures, or surgery. Their personal boundary space is trespassed repeatedly during examination and treatment. The intimate details of their sexual activities become part of an impersonal medical record. In order to comply with treatment demands, the partners must focus on what they have failed to accomplish. There is no balance in their lives, as they neglect other goals and needs (Mahlstedt, 1985). Most patients feel that they have lost control of their lives and their bodies. In a comparison of 73 infertile couples and 73 fertile couples, Christie (1980) found that the infertile couples viewed themselves as externally, rather than internally, controlled. Indeed, the infertile become subject to the plans and therapeutic goals of the infertility team, as well as vulnerable to the roller coaster ride of emotions inherent in infertility treatment.

Despite their perception of external control, couples undergoing infertility treatment are faced with daily decision making. As treatment progresses, choices range from continuing to take basal body temperatures, to participating further in what often seem fruitless efforts to conceive, to undergoing additional diagnostic or therapeutic modalities. Treatment is sometimes protracted, but there is no guarantee of success. The optimism and dedication required to continue treatment are repeatedly dashed by the appearance of monthly menses, thus, frustration and depression are frequently a cyclic occurrence. Continued treatment may strain a couple's coping abilities, interpersonal relationships, and financial resources, but the decision to cease treatment requires recognition and acceptance of the finality of permanent infertility.

Couples revolve through the feelings of surprise, denial, anger, isolation, and grief at each decision point. Partners generally do not get into crisis at the same time, or the family system would collapse. Paradoxically, because the dysfunctional partner may not realize that the functional partner is striving for equilibrium, the dysfunctional partner may interpret the incongruence as evidence that the other cannot understand feelings or problems. It is often at this point that the couple seeks outside help.

Gender differences seem to influence perceptions of infertility. Infertile wives are reported to suffer more significant damage to self-esteem and to marital, sexual, and life satisfaction (Bernstein, Potts, & Matto, 1985; Link & Darling, 1986; Rutledge, 1979). Women have reported feeling more feminine and sexually attractive shortly after surgery for infertility treatment. Even post–tubal ligation patients have described reproductive fantasies up to 1 year after surgery. It appears that, as long as motherhood is even theoretically possible, a woman feels intact as "female of the species" (Hertz, 1982). Wives whose husbands did not participate in the infertility evaluation and treatment had the lowest level of life satisfaction (Bernstein et al., 1985). Infertile men are reported to have more intense feelings of guilt, anger, frustration, and isolation than do infertile women, but both feel increased guilt and blame (Bernstein et al., 1985). Compared with fertile couple controls, infertile couples showed wide discrepancies between their perceptions of their current selves and their perceptions of their ideal and parent selves (Christie, 1980). Perhaps with the evolution of women's roles in society, gender differences may not be quite as marked in the future.

Infertility cannot be treated like other illnesses, because it deals with the essence of maleness and femaleness (Kaufman, 1969). Treatment can reinforce sexual insecurities and doubts (Hertz, 1982). The power balance of sexual initiation and refusal patterns gives way to sexual "performances" that are medically dictated. It becomes the woman's job to arrange intercourse at the right time and the man's job to carry through intercourse with or without sexual desire (Lalos et al., 1985).

Sex on schedule can increase a couple's stress. Men may develop impotence (frequently midcycle), ejaculatory dysfunction (ranging from premature ejaculation to anejaculation), excessive or diminished sexual frequency, and decreased or no libido (Berger, 1977, 1980; Rutledge, 1979; Seibel & Taymor, 1982). Reportedly, 10% of infertility may be partially or completely attributable to such male sexual dysfunction (Amelar et al., 1977), and this dysfunction could be a stress response to findings of oligospermia or the sexual demands of the infertility evaluation (Berger, 1980). Women may experience vaginismus, anorgasmia, and decreased or no libido (Berger, 1977; Rutledge, 1979; Seibel & Taymor, 1982). The couple may be unable to achieve coitus for a postcoital examination. The widespread practice of informing the wife of semen analysis outcomes further contributes to sexual pressures. Infertile couples followed 2 years after infertility surgery reported a continued deterioration in sexual satisfaction (Lalos et al., 1985).

The relationship of patients with the health care team is critical. If the patients perceive the team as competent and supportive of them as individuals (not just cases), the infertile have one less area of conflict in their treatment experience. The couple and the health care team can have common goals, a common "enemy," and shared rules by which to resolve conflicts. If communication and rapport are diminished, the relationship disintegrates into an "us" vs. "them" conflict. This relegates the health care team to the ranks of pregnant women and tactless acquaintances who generally collect the frustration and anger of the infertile. Such a relationship creates a win-or-lose situation in which the infertile couple is ultimately the loser.

At times, despite good communication and rapport, treatment failure strains the relationship between patients and staff. Generally, there are two patient responses, enmeshment or distancing, with anger and depression the ultimate outcomes of each. Frequently lacking other social support, the infertile couple may become enmeshed with staff members and overly dependent on them. On the other hand, patients may distance themselves from the staff because they feel betrayed or have no more energy to pursue treatment, paradoxically making it impossible to establish new goals, such as termination of treatment.

The health care team may demonstrate the same behaviors of enmeshment and distancing with patients who fail to become pregnant. Enmeshment may be evidenced in a flurry of attempted treatments that have very low probabilities of success. Staff members may create distance between themselves and these patients by being less available for appointments or less supportive. This dance of intimacy between patients and staff is obviously complex, but the nature of infertility treatment increases its occurrence. The involvement of the family therapist as an integral member of the infertility health care team is especially beneficial in confronting this issue.

ALTERNATIVE INFERTILITY TREATMENTS

In the past decade, couples that fail to achieve pregnancy through traditional infertility treatment methods have had available artificial insemination by donor (AID) and in vitro fertilization (IVF) procedures. Both AID and IVF patients are faced with special medical risks, as well as emotional, legal, and moral pressures.

Couples whose infertility is the result of a male factor (e.g., azoospermia, severe oligospermia, poor sperm penetration) may achieve pregnancy through AID. These couples must accept and cope with the fact that the wife is inseminated by a health care professional and subsequently bears a child whose biological father is another male. In order to accept this, they often must examine their definitions of parenthood, maleness, and marital fidelity.

Couples infertile for varying reasons may benefit from IVF. Today, the procedure is commonly used to treat fallopian tube disease that is not responsive or amenable to surgical repair, endometriosis resistant to therapy, persistent male factor infertility, and unexplained infertility. In some cases of male factor infertility, IVF may involve the use of donor sperm; couples electing to use donor semen for IVF confront the same issues that those undergoing AID confront. In addition, IVF demands special physical, financial and time commitments. Patients who undergo IVF often have extensive infertility treatment histories and tend to be knowledgeable and compliant patients, however, they consider IVF the "end of the line" of treatment alternatives. Although couples are hopeful and excited by the promise of "high-tech" pregnancies, they must simultaneously face the strong probability of intense disappointment. In vitro fertilization is unsuccessful in the majority of cycle attempts. When Freeman, Boxer, Rickels, Tureck, and Mastroianni (1985) examined the plans of IVF patients should they not become pregnant, they found that 55% had no plans, and 32% planned to investigate adoption, foster parenting, or surrogate pregnancy. Four percent had educational plans. Nine percent designated other plans.

INFERTILITY RESOLUTION

Grief work is mandatory in the resolution of infertility. Mahlstedt (1985) related the infertility experience to losses in adulthood that have the greatest significance in the etiology of depression. Included were the loss of a relationship, health, status or prestige, self-esteem, self-confidence, security, or important fantasy fulfillment, and the loss of something or someone of great symbolic value. Mahlstedt aptly concluded that, while any of these losses could individually precipitate a depressive reaction, infertility involves all of them. Because of the intangibility of their loss, infertile couples are at risk for delayed grief recovery.

Those unable to conceive may exhibit dysfunctional coping methods similar to the avoidance, obliteration, and idolization that Crosby and Jose (1983) reported in many families following the death of a family member. Avoidance involves diverting thoughts and feelings away from the loss and lengthens the denial process. Mahlstedt (1985) compared grief for the loss resulting from infertility to that for a soldier missing in action. Nothing is definite in either case, and hope enables survivors to avoid the pain. Patients with unexplained infertility are especially vulnerable to the use of avoidance. Idolization is the process of making the absent child more perfect than the child realistically could have been in actual life. The fantasized family experience is unrivaled by ordinary living. Toys, clothing, and furniture waiting for the never conceived or lost child may be saved and endowed with even greater significance. In order to resolve their grief, however, infertile couples must come to terms with the loss and emptiness associated with the absent baby and its family role.

Obliteration is an attempt to dispose of all memory traces and fantasies of the absent child or childbearing attempts. Exceeding denial and avoidance in severity, obliteration involves living as though the desire for a child never existed. If even one member of the couple uses this coping method, the system is likely to close down, at least temporarily.

Resolution of infertility involves successfully acknowledging, expressing, and dealing with the emotional responses to infertility. Sexuality, self-image, and self-esteem must be disconnected from childbearing (Menning, 1980). Couples must decide how they wish to restructure their family system. Some may have formed family boundaries centered so rigidly around the desired child that they find it frightening to reevaluate their marital relationship and terminate the infertility treatment cycle when the clinician recommends that they do so. Patterns of decision making and power in their relationship may be altered by the transition state.

Alternative paths to parenthood may be pursued through adoption or surrogate parenting. Some couples may choose to redefine their life goals to exclude parenting. Some motivations for having a child (e.g., fulfillment of traditional role expectations or solution for marital problems) may be resolved so that needs are met in different ways. Making a choice requires emotional, economic, and social adaptation. Failure to adapt can prevent the successful progression through the family life cycle.

Frequently, it is only when the infertile couple has adjusted to nonparent-hood or has attained parenthood (even through adoption) that intense dis-appointment can be acknowledged (Hertz, 1982). Some studies have noted that adoptive parents' psychological reactions to infertility correlate with their psychological ability to parent a child (Cooper, 1971; Toussieng, 1962; Wiehe, 1976). In a follow-up study of adopted boys, Christie (1980) found the adoptive mothers' inability to accept their own infertility correlated with the later emergence of hypochondriacal concerns in their adoptive sons. Andrews (1970) found that the ability of adoptive mothers to discuss their feelings about their infertility correlated significantly with their later ability to explain the fact of adoption to their children.

Adoption may symbolize reproductive inadequacy, and the presence of the child may act as a narcissistic injury among couples who have not yet worked through conflicts in their feelings toward infertility. Failure to deal with their unresolved feelings about their infertility may interfere with parents' ability to become close to the adopted child (Rosenfeld & Mitchell, 1979). When one adoptive parent has resolved these feelings and the other has not, the resolved parent and the adopted child may form a family coalition, leaving the unre-solved parent in isolation. Similar difficulties may result from other methods of parenthood.

MARITAL COUNSELING RECOMMENDATIONS

Marriage counselors who work with the infertile need a basic knowledge of the medical aspects of infertility assessment and treatment in order to under-stand and appreciate fully the stresses placed on the individual and couple in this process. Each of the five major stages of the process has particular stressors for the infertile couple and, thus, specific counseling intervention require-ments:

1. Recognition of Infertility and Desire for Treatment

   - exploration of current conflicts and stressors that may influence the couple's desire for a child
   - discussion of the couple's individual and mutual fertility desires and the congruency of these desires
   - exploration of myths used to explain infertility
   - facilitation of the couple's ability to cope with the "crisis of infertility" and education that their feelings are normal responses

- discussion of fears and notions about what infertility evaluation and treatment will involve
- investigation of formal and informal support systems and recommendations for their use

2. Infertility Evaluation

- self-image evaluation in terms of sexuality, feelings of failure, and physical well-being associated with infertility
- investigation of the identified patient's fears (e.g., guilt, abandonment, failure), as well as feelings of exclusion by the other spouse
- identification of decision-making patterns of the couple and their satisfaction with these patterns

3. Infertility Treatment

- exploration of individual coping styles and their influence on the couple
- evaluation of the ways in which the couple provides mutual support
- discussion of the couple's feelings that they are out of control vs. their ability to balance their lives despite the hassles of infertility treatment
- identification of the couple's definition of the duration and termination point of treatment
- investigation and discussion of the couple's comfort and efficacy in dealing with health care team
- exploration of the effects of treatments on the couple (e.g., sexuality, life satisfaction, economic and social functioning)

4. Alternative infertility treatment

- facilitation of resolution of emotional, legal, ethical, medical risk, economic, and time commitment issues
- preparation for infertility treatment termination and resolution

5. Infertility resolution

- facilitation of grief process
- assistance in restructuring goals of family to include different parenting alternatives vs. different life goals

Exhibit 1 Infertility Psychosocial Assessment

I.   Complete sexual history
      A. Frequency and response
      B. Function/dysfunction
      C. Religious or ethnic influence on sexual patterns
      D. Past sexual history
            1. Function/dysfunction
            2. Abortion/pregnancy
            3. Sexually transmitted diseases
            4. Prior sperm donor/surrogate mother
            5. Homosexual or ambisexual patterns
      E. Extramarital relationships
      F. Changes in any sexuality patterns secondary to infertility or treatment process
II.   Mental status
      A. Psychiatric history
      B. Current medical status (e.g., symptoms of depression, anxiety)
III. Relationship status
      A. Current satisfaction/dissatisfaction
      B. Perceived relationship strengths and weaknesses
      C. Traditional decision-making methods
      D. Past history of marital discord/therapy
      E. History of prior marriages/divorces
      F. Individual coping mechanisms used in dealing with stress
IV.   Fertility choice
      A. Who brought the couple in for infertility evaluation?
      B. How does the other spouse regard the desire for fertility? Is fertility a mutual goal?
      C. Does the couple have children together from prior fertility or from other relationships?
      D. What needs will fertility fulfill?
      E. Are there myths about the role of a child in the family?
      F. Does the couple have beliefs/myths about the etiology of infertility?
      G. What ambivalencies toward fertility exist?
      H. What is each partner's career involvement, and how will fertility influence career goals?
V.   Extended family stressors
      A. Are children necessary to fulfill traditional role obligations?
      B. Is there a relationship in fertility planning/timing across generations?
      C. Are there recent deaths or births in the family?
VI.   Change
      A. Prior to the infertility evaluation history, were there any changes in sexuality/relationships, career, family, life style, or personal beliefs that have changed the couple's interaction patterns?
      B. Is infertility a symptom that allows the couple to seek treatment for family dysfunction?
VII. Infertility adaptation
      A. Does the couple have any support systems to help them deal with their infertility?
      B. Is the couple satisfied with their health care team's ability to educate them about treatment and give them support?

Exhibit 1 continued

C. What treatment choices have the couple made at this point?
D. Is the couple realistic in their expectations of infertility treatment (e.g., "When I get pregnant . . .")?
E. Have the couple discussed the point at which they will terminate treatment?
F. Is a primary goal of infertility treatment to relieve guilt?
G. Is the couple able to communicate and support individual ways to cope with infertility?
H. Is there a change in mental status or an exacerbation of prior psychiatric symptoms?
I. Does the couple's life revolve around aspects of infertility?
J. Are problems secondary to infertility developing (e.g., employment difficulties secondary to repeated medical appointments, financial drain, individual dysfunction secondary to stress, depression, lack of geographical mobility in order to complete treatment with a particular medical center)?
K. Have individual or couple self-concepts changed during the infertility process?
L. Have there been any changes in the couple's sexuality/relationships, career, family, life style, or personal beliefs that have affected their interaction patterns since the infertility evaluation/treatment began?

- promotion of successful termination of relationship with infertility health care team
- re-formation of self-concept without traditional parenthood

If the couple has not resolved stressors that arose before they reached their current stage, intervention must begin with aspects of the stage in which adaptation was arrested. The Infertility Psychosocial Assessment (Exhibit 1) assists the marriage counselor in discovering each couple's unique stress profile and speed of adaptation.

Joining the family system by using Minuchin's basic approach of education, support, and guidance allows the marriage counselor to ensure that the couple are aware of their goals and their adaptation throughout the process of infertility evaluation and treatment (Minuchin, 1974). Time invested in assessing system dynamics is well spent, as the family therapist can better grasp family roles, communication patterns, and component desires for fertility by using a systems perspective. If family system disequilibrium is the primary cause of infertility, the couple and the therapist can deal with the disequilibrium immediately and perhaps avoid biological clinical interventions. At any rate, beginning the infertility evaluation process with congruent goals and expectations can help unite the couple in dealing with ambivalencies about pregnancy and upcoming stresses, perhaps averting their subsequent withdrawal from the evaluation process. The counselor's role is not to form value judgments about the validity of the couple's goal of pregnancy, but to ensure that the couple are aware of the system dynamics that contribute to this goal. If infertility treatment does not result in pregnancy, the couple must consider alternatives. The family therapist must recognize that the family system has reached some sort of homeostasis throughout the infertility treatment process and must again change at this point.

REFERENCES

Allison, J.R. (1979). Roles and role conflict of women in infertile couples. *Psychology of Women Quarterly, 4*(1), 97–133.

Andrews, R.G. (1970). Adoption and the resolution of infertility. *Fertility and Sterility, 21,* 73–84.

Amelar, R.D., Dublen, L., & Walsh, P.C. (1977). *Male infertility* (pp. 202–203). Philadelphia: W.B. Saunders.

Aronson, H.G., & Glienke, C.F. (1963). A study of the incidence of pregnancy following adoption. *Fertility and Sterility, 15,* 547–553.

Banks, A.L. (1965). Counseling in infertility problems. In R.H. Klemer (Ed.), *Counseling in marital and sexual problems: A physician's handbook.* Baltimore: Williams & Wilkins.

Benedek, T. (1952). Infertility as a psychologic defense. *Fertility and Sterility, 3,* 527–537.

Bents, H. (1985). Psychology of male infertility—A literature survey. *International Journal of Andrology, 8,* 325–336.

Berger, D.M. (1977). The role of the psychiatrist in a reproductive biology clinic. *Fertility and Sterility, 28*(2), 141–143.

Berger, D.M. (1980). Infertility: A psychiatrist's perspective. *Canadian Journal of Psychiatry, 25*(7), 553–559.

Bernstein, J., Potts, N., & Mattox, J.H. (Nov/Dec. 1985) Assessment of psychological dysfunction associated with infertility. *Journal of Obstetrics and Gynecology Nursing,* (Suppl. 63–66).

Brand, H.J. (1982). Psychological stress and infertility: Part 2. Psychometric test data. *British Journal of Medical Psychology, 55,* 385–388.

Christie, G.L. (1980). The psychological and social management of the infertile couple. In. R.J. Pepperell, B. Hudson, & C. Wood (Eds.), *The infertile couple* (pp. 229–247). New York: Churchill Livingstone.

Cooper, H. (1971). Psychogenic infertility and adoption. *South African Medical Journal, 12,* 719–722.

Crosby, J.F., & Jose, N.L. (1983). Death: Family adjustment to loss. In C. Figley (Ed.), *Stress and the family: Coping with catastrophe* (Vol. 2, pp. 76–89). New York: Brunner/Mazel.

Denber, H.C. (1978). Psychiatric aspects of infertility. *The Journal of Reproductive Medicine, 20,* 23–29.

El-Minawi, M.F., Abdel-Hadi, H., Ibraham, A.A., & Wahby, O. (1978). Comparative evaluation of laparoscopy and hysterosalpingography in infertile patients. *Obstetrics and Gynaecology, 59,* 29–37.

Freeman, E.W., Boxer, A.S., Rickels, K., Tureck, R., & Mastroianni, L., Jr. (1985). Psychological evaluation and support in a program of in vitro fertilization and embryo transfer. *Fertility and Sterility, 43,* 48–53.

Griffin, M.E. (1983). Resolving infertility: An emotional crisis. *ARON Journal, 38*, 597–601.

Hertz, D.G. (1982). Infertility and the physician-patient relationship: A biopsychosocial challenge. *General Hospital Psychiatry, 4*, 95–101.

Kaufman, S.A. (1969). Impact of infertility on the marital and sexual relationship. *Fertility and Sterility, 20*, 380–383.

Keye, W.R., Deneris, A., Butell, S., Wilson, T., & Sullivan, J. (1983). Predicting women's emotional response to infertility. *Fertility and Sterility, 39*(3), 417.

Klemer, R.H., Rutherford, R.N., Banks, A.L., & Coburn, W.A. (1966). Marital counseling with the infertile couple. *Fertility and Sterility, 17*(1), 104–109.

Kraft, A.D., Palombo, M.A., Mitchell, D., Dean, C., Meyers, S., & Schmidt, A. (1980). The psychological dimensions of infertility. *American Journal of Orthopsychiatry, 50*(4), 618–628.

Lalos, A., Lalos, O., Jacobsson, L., & von Schoultz, B. (1985). A psychological reaction to the medical investigation and surgical treatment of infertility. *Gynecologic-Obstetrical Investigation, 20*, 209–217.

Link, P.W., & Darling, C.A. (1986). Couples undergoing treatment for infertility: Dimensions of life satisfaction. *Journal of Sex and Marital Therapy, 12*, 46–59.

Mahlstedt, P.P. (1985). The psychological component of infertility. *Fertility and Sterility, 43*, 335–345.

Matthews, R., & Matthews, A.N. (1986). Infertility and involuntary childlessness: The transition of nonparenthood. *Journal of Marriage and the Family, 48*, 641–649.

McCartney, C. (1985). The doctor-patient relationship in infertility treatment. In M.G. Hammond & L.M. Talbert (Eds.), *Infertility—A practical guide for the physician* (pp. 15–24). Oradell, NJ: Medical Economics Books.

Menning, B.E. (1979). Counseling infertile couples. *Contemporary Ob/Gyn, 13*, 101–139.

Menning, B.E. (1980). The emotional needs of infertile couples. *Fertility and Sterility, 34*(4), 313–319.

Minuchin, S. (1974). *Families and family therapy* (pp. 123–137). Cambridge, MA: Harvard University Press.

Murphy, M.J. (1984). Birth timing and marital breakdown: A reinterpretation of the evidence. *Journal of Biosocial Science, 16*, 487–500.

Noyes, R.W., & Chapnick, E.M. (1964). Literature on psychology and infertility. *Fertility and Sterility, 15*, 543–558.

Rosenfeld, D.L., & Mitchell, E. (1979). Treating the emotional aspects of infertility: Counseling services in an infertility clinic. *American Journal of Obstetrics and Gynecology, 135*(2), 177–180.

Rutledge, A.L. (1979). Psychomarital evaluation and treatment of the infertile couple. *Clinical Obstetrics and Gynecology, 22*(1), 255–267.

Seibel, M.M., & Taymor, M.L. (1982). Emotional aspects of infertility. *Fertility and Sterility, 37*(2), 137–145.

Toussieng, P.W. (1962). Psychological problems of adoptees. *Child Welfare, 41*, 59–65.

Tyler, E.T. (1960). Occurrence of pregnancy following adoption. *Fertility and Sterility, 11*, 581–589.

Wiehe, V.R. (1976). Psychological reaction to infertility. *Psychology Reprints, 38*, 863–866.

2. Stress in Kidney Recipients and Their Families

Diane Logan Thompson, PhD
Assistant Professor
Counselor Education and Family Practice
University of Iowa

S ince 1954, when the first clinically successful kidney transplantation in the United States was performed, the surgical and medical complexities of kidney transplantation have decreased, and the rate of patient survival has increased. Concurrently, interest in the psychosocial responses of transplant patients and their families has grown (Abram & Buchanan, 1976; Basch, 1973). Family therapists are more and more frequently being called upon to work with families who are experiencing stress related to end-stage renal disease in one of their members.

RECIPIENTS

> . . . the events to follow, and our reactions to these events, could be graphed as the curves in a wave, a huge tidal wave in our lives first continuing downward, a slow descent to the bottom, before sky-rocketing up to a crest and then leveling off again at sea level. I can now see these stages clearly but at the time never knew exactly what was to come next or how we would effectively deal with each event. (Lohr, 1981, p. 56)

Preoperative Issues

Before they even contemplate the possibility of a kidney transplant, most potential recipients have experienced considerable physical and psychosocial stress related to renal failure and dialysis. At times, the onset of renal failure is sudden and unexpected, precipitating a grieflike reaction in the patients. Dialysis patients are continuously confronted with the physical sensations of illness, an uncertain prognosis, and the threat of death. It becomes virtually impossible for them to predict how they will feel at any one point in time or to plan for the future.

Dialysis itself involves absolute dependence on an artificial kidney and produces a variety of psychophysical effects, including apathy, drowsiness, inability to concentrate, restlessness, ability to tolerate only brief periods of activity, irritability, depression, and cognitive impairment. Severe dietary and fluid restrictions demand further alterations in the patient's life style. Inability to maintain employment may create significant financial problems and loss of status (Simmons, Klein, & Simmons, 1977). Children on dialysis are generally delayed in social, emotional, and physical development. As a result of the handicap imposed by their kidney disease, they often feel isolated, depressed, inadequate, and excessively dependent on their parents (Glass & Hickerson, 1976; Sampson, 1975).

Despite these difficulties, many patients develop close relationships with the staff of the dialysis unit and feel comfortable with the treatment that they are receiving. They may be initially ambivalent about transplantation, because leaving the dialysis unit is like leaving their home (Carosella, 1984). Prior experience with dialysis may actually facilitate a patient's adjustment to transplantation, however. Freyberger (1980) discovered that patients who had learned to trust the medical staff of their dialysis center were able to transfer this trust to transplant surgeons and surgical nurses. Furthermore, because of their frequent hospitalizations in the past, they did not find the hospital atmosphere foreign or threatening.

There are two major contraindications for kidney transplantation: (1) moderately severe mental retardation and (2) untreatable psychosis. Psychosocial screening for patient selection should include consideration of the willingness of the patient to cooperate with treatment, as well as any self-destructive tendencies of the patient. For example, it has been suggested that some potential kidney recipients unconsciously see transplantation as a quick means to death (Knight, 1980). In these cases, it is the task of the treatment staff to discover what motivates the patient to live and to move him or her in that direction before the transplant procedure.

After a potential kidney recipient has been selected, the search for a donor begins. Current statistics regarding transplants from deceased individuals and those from living family members should be presented to the patient at this time. The donor search may create considerable stress and anxiety for patients. Those who are waiting for a cadaver donor find themselves hoping and waiting for someone to die a sudden, tragic death. In addition, not knowing if or when a cadaver donor will be found may be frustrating and disrupts their life style, as they must always be "on call" (Buchanan, 1975).

Patients who hope to receive a kidney from a living related donor may perceive themselves as a burden to the family (Buchanan, 1975). On the other hand, they may refuse to accept a kidney from a particular potential donor for fear of feeling obligated to that person (Stewart, 1983). Family members, particularly those who do not wish to donate a kidney, may not communicate directly with the patients, who are then left with the additional stress and uncertainty of not knowing whether they should be placed on the waiting list for a cadaver donor (Simmons & Klein, 1972). In his observations of potential kidney recipients between 10 and 18 years of age, Sampson (1975) noted mild depressive reactions that fluctuated with the rate at which potential donors were evaluated. Wenzl (1975) recommended involving pediatric patients, aged 10 and older, in discussions related to the donor search, as they are generally well able to comprehend their status and the threat of death.

The awareness that their life may depend on the kindness and generosity of a family member may be particularly stressful for some patients. Many react with pain and anger when family members are ambivalent or refuse to donate a kidney to them. In order to avoid such pain, patients may use denial or repression, or they may simply accept the nondonor's reasons for the decision. Others may, at least temporarily, become bitter and angry (Simmons, Klein, & Simmons, 1977).

Thorough preoperative preparation of the kidney recipient, both medically and psychosocially, reduces the number of problems likely to arise after transplantation. A potential kidney recipient is initially enthusiastic and eager to talk with the transplantation staff. At this early stage of the transplantation process, the staff should determine what a kidney transplant means to the patient. For example, some patients fantasize that a "new kidney" will make them a "new person" (i.e., better and healthier), and they do not want to hear the more realistic facts about the risks of surgery and the postoperative limitations (Sampson, 1975). Some patients believe that they will be "reborn" after the transplantation, while others feel that transplantation involves stealing an organ from a donor who may return for it (Knight, 1980).

Patients' predialysis level of functioning and ability to cope with stress may be used as predictors of their ability to cope with the stress of transplantation and possible kidney rejection. While the use of some denial may help patients to move beyond their anxiety and apprehension regarding the risks of transplant surgery, extreme denial may signal the need to delay surgery until the patients can discuss their fears and concerns more realistically (Carosella, 1984).

As the time for transplantation approaches, patients may begin to feel elation, coupled with more stress and anxiety; they may be more willing to discuss facts related to the surgery with the transplantation staff (Sampson, 1975). The fact that kidney recipients are not out of danger or released from medical care following the transplantation should be reemphasized, as this has been found to contribute to the development of more realistic goals. Specific patient concerns, such as the fear of death or kidney rejection, doubts regarding the ability to function normally (i.e., outside the sick role) again, issues concerning the effects of a kidney from an opposite sex donor, or guilt related to the inability ever to repay a donor, should be addressed at this time (Buchanan, 1975; Fielding, 1972; Knight, 1980).

Postoperative Issues

The purpose of kidney transplantation is to improve significantly the physical, psychosocial, and vocational functioning of the kidney recipient. Following a successful transplantation, patients are released from fluid restrictions and any dependence on dialysis. Diet restrictions are reduced. Although the patient is required to remain on medication indefinitely, this is generally not a major issue (Freyberger, 1980).

Having survived the crisis of end-stage renal failure and major surgery, kidney recipients are generally happier and demonstrate a greater appreciation of life than ever before. At 1 year post-transplantation, they report increased levels of satisfaction with the occupational, recreational, and social areas of their lives; the majority have returned to most of their previous activities, including socializing more with friends and returning to full-time employment (Simmons, Klein, & Simmons, 1977). Unlike dialysis patients, who see the end of part of their normal life style, transplant patients have the hope of a new life (Freyberger, 1980). Patient comments contain themes of rebirth and rededication (Abram & Buchanan, 1976).

"In most cases, a successful kidney transplant is the best psychotherapy for anyone in renal failure, whatever their psychiatric problems" (Eisendrath, 1976, p. 385). Improvements have been reported in body image (Knight, 1980) and self-esteem. Depression and anxiety have been noted to decrease, and impotence has been reported to disappear. The intensity of defense mechanisms, such as secondary hypochondria, partial infantile regression, and denial, have also been said to decrease (Freyberger, 1980). In addition, Simmons, Klein, and Simmons (1977) noted that patients were less preoccupied with themselves, while seeing themselves as more independent and in control of their lives. Female patients tended to demonstrate greater adjustment 1 year post-transplantation than did male patients. Topor (1981) highlighted the physical, psychological, and social improvements of preschool and preadolescent children following kidney transplantation.

For some patients, however, the stress of long-term chronic illness creates significant psychological problems that are not immediately overcome by surgery. There may be social barriers in the vocational rehabilitation of patients who perceive themselves as well, but may be perceived by others as ill. Furthermore, new forms of stress may develop following transplantation. The occurrence of postoperative complications, such as bleeding, infection, and urinary leakage, may increase the likelihood of kidney rejection and a return to dialysis. The immunosuppressive drugs may have side-effects, such as muscle deterioration, redistribution of body and facial fat (e.g., "moon face" and "Cushingoid" appearance), acne, impotence, numbness in the extremities, bone damage, hair loss, cataracts, and mood disturbances. Long-term prognosis remains uncertain, and the patient may find it difficult psychologically to accept a body part from another individual.

The most common psychiatric complication following transplant surgery is depression (Buchanan, 1975; Knight, 1980; Sampson, 1975; Stewart, 1983). It generally occurs secondary to physical complications, painful treatment, drug therapy, fear of death, unresolved grief related to the loss of an organ (Abram & Buchanan, 1976); perceived lack of control over the dimensions of life outside treatment (Devins, Binik, Hollomby, Barre, & Guttman, 1981); guilt and feelings of having taken advantage of the donor, fear that the donor may die (Kemph, 1966); and, among adolescent recipients, hampered social skills in heterosexual relationships (Topor, 1981). Stress is generally highest soon after transplant surgery, when the risk of rejection is greatest and the steroid dosage is highest (Simmons, Klein, & Simmons, 1977).

The patient's premorbid personality, history, present situation, and perception of the treatability of transplant complications or side-effects influence the patient's ability to cope with the transplantation process (Fielding, 1972). Patients most likely to develop psychosocial complications include men, persons who have a low income and little education, those whose adjustment to prior stress was poor, those whose appearance has been affected by the administration of steroids, those who receive less support from their family or who felt rejected by their spouse prior to transplantation, and those who have problems in their relationship with the donor 1 year after surgery (Simmons, Klein, & Simmons, 1977).

Caution must be used in interpreting data from patients with physical symptoms. For example, Simmons, Klein and Simmons (1977) reported that, although kidney receipients who took the Minnesota Multiphasic Personality Inventory (MMPI) showed significant improvement on emotional adjustment following transplant surgery, they still indicated more problems in many areas than did a group of normal controls. The authors emphasized, however, that these findings may reflect the disease process rather than emotional maladjustment, because scales 1, 2, 3, and 8 of the MMPI include items on physical complaints. In fact, kidney recipients who identified themselves as individuals with health problems 1 year following transplant surgery showed greater maladjustment than did healthier patients on six of the seven MMPI scales.

FAMILY

The stress and anxiety created by end-stage renal failure and kidney transplantation are experienced not only by the patient, but also by the patient's family. The onset of any catastrophic or chronic illness may create a crisis for the family. Family members generally require a considerable degree of psychological competence and social skills, as they may need to assume new roles, either temporarily or permanently. The illness may magnify family dynamics and highlight family problems. Interrupted employment may create financial crises and change the family's social status within the community. Family members may feel isolated and may find it difficult to meet each other's needs for intimacy and support; there may be little time or energy for them to meet these needs in relationships outside the family (Fife, 1985).

McCubbin, McCubbin, Patterson, Cauble, Wilson, and Warwick (1983) identified four primary tasks of families in crisis:

1. coping directly with the stress and related events
2. maintaining family stability
3. keeping anxiety within tolerable limits
4. obtaining social supports from extended family and the community

Such tasks require the family to communicate openly and to negotiate with some sense of flexibility. Otherwise, the family is at risk for the development of a variety of secondary problems, such as role strain and role conflict. Fife (1985) suggested that rigid role complementarity in the absence of role reciprocity leads to role diffusion and disorganization in times of crisis.

End-stage renal failure and kidney transplantation are particularly difficult for the family because of the ongoing uncertainty of the illness (e.g., infection, possible organ rejection, or other complications) and the high dependence of the patient on the family (Cain & Staver, 1976). Family members often have a grieflike reaction, similar to that of the patient, following the onset of renal failure. Not only must they adapt to sudden, changing roles, but also they must deal with the ill person, who is often withdrawn, irritable, and moody. The patient's decreased interest in sex and/or impotence may contribute to sexual frustration and increase marital stress, and the constant threat of death is felt by all (Cramond, 1971; Simmons, Klein, & Simmons, 1977).

At the beginning of the pretransplantation evaluation process, the patient is informed of the desirability of transplanting a kidney from a living relative. Recruitment of a donor is then often left to the family. The donor search may generate considerable anxiety, guilt (in those who do not want to be the donor), a sense of obligation, uncertainty, and fear within the family (Payne & Harrison, 1984). Donor nephrectomy (i.e., removal of a kidney from a donor) is a major surgical procedure, and the family may fear the consequences of surgery for the donor. Family members may disagree on the best candidate for donor. They may refuse to consider certain members for donor because of their personal and family responsibilities or their involvement in previous family conflicts. For example, they may exclude the family "black sheep" on the ground that he or she could use donation for personal benefit, such as returning to the good graces of the family (Musial, 1980; Simmons, Klein, & Simmons, 1977). On the other hand, the family may select as donor the member whom they are least likely to miss (Schumann, 1974).

There are few norms to guide the family in the decision on a kidney donor. If the patient is a child, the donor selection process may be much less stressful for the family, because there are clear cultural expectations that parents should sacrifice for their children. In fact, parents are the most likely relatives to volunteer and among the least ambivalent donors. If the patient is an adult, however, the selection of a donor is more difficult. The obligation of adult siblings to one another or of adult children to their parents is much less clear. Although adult siblings are generally the best genetic match for kidney donation, they may be caught between obligations to two families—their family of origin and their family of procreation (Simmons, Klein, & Simmons, 1977). Knight (1980) suggested that siblings' obligation to their spouse and children generally takes precedence over their duty to their brother or sister. Higgerson and Bulechek (1982) identified only one case in which there was conflict between the donor's birth family and marital family, however.

Simmons, Klein, and Simmons (1977) described two stages in the donor selection process: (1) the request stage and (2) the response stage. During the request stage, relatives may be told to donate, asked to donate, or just informed of the need for a donor. Those who are told or asked to donate may feel pressured (Knight, 1980; Schumann, 1974). Of the donors studied by Simmons, Klein, and Simmons (1977), 6% perceived themselves as "subject to undue family pressure," while independent coders rated 11% as under significant family pressure. Similarly, 4% of the donors interviewed by Higgerson and Bulechek (1982) said that they felt direct pressure from their families to donate, and 15% "agreed a little" that they felt pressure to donate.

The majority of potential donors are not asked directly to donate. They are told only that the patient must undergo a kidney transplant, and it is assumed that they will understand that a donor is needed. In some cases, they are told of the need for a related kidney donor. This indirect communication may place less pressure on family members, allowing them to decide if they wish to volunteer, but it may not convey a clear message. Failing to understand the urgency, family members may not respond, and the patient may misinterpret this as a refusal (Simmons, Klein, & Simmons, 1977).

Rather than directly contacting each family member, most patients approach one person who, in turn, informs the other family members of the need for a kidney donor. The intermediary is often a parent or spouse (Fellner, 1971; Simmons, Hickey, Kjellstrand, & Simmons, 1971; Simmons, Klein, & Simmons, 1977; Stewart, 1983). Although spouses are generally most eager to donate, the fact that they are not biologically related makes them ineligible. They are, however, in a position to place some pressure on others to donate, as they are not asking others to do something that they would be unwilling to do themselves. At the same time, it is less uncomfortable for family members to refuse another relative than to refuse the patient directly (Musial, 1980; Schumann, 1974).

During the response stage, no response is common; 30% of the eligible relatives studied by Simmons, Klein, and Simmons (1977) did not respond. This creates additional stress for the patient, as it may delay transplantation and fosters emotional distance between the patient and the family at a time when support is needed. It gives family members more time to make their decision, however. If they decide not to donate, their failure to respond avoids directly hurting or insulting the patient (Simmons, Klein, & Simmons, 1977).

Those who are most likely to donate a kidney are (1) parents; (2) relatives who still share a household and siblings who are close in age and of the same sex as the potential recipient; (3) those with higher education and occupational status and younger age than those less likely to donate; (4) those who are the only possible donor in the family of origin and those who generally take greater family responsibility than do others; and (5) relatives who are emotionally tied to the patient and who live in geographical proximity to the patient (Simmons, Klein, & Simmons, 1977). Families that have more than one eligible donor may use the deliberation model for donor selection. Such a model includes a consideration of sex, age, ambivalence, matching, and family objections (Higgerson & Bulechek, 1982). Simmons, Klein, and Simmons (1977) found that, in 15% of the families studied, the donor was selected by individual family members or by the medical staff rather than through explicit family discussion. In another 58% of the cases, family members participated in a conscious, deliberate donor selection process and generally reached agreement by consensus (Simmons, Klein, & Simmons, 1977).

Nondonors (i.e., family members who are eligible to donate, but do not volunteer) are reportedly less emotionally close to kidney recipients than are donors and have greater obligations to their family of procreation. Many resent the pressure to donate that they perceive their family to be placing on them. Family members, in turn, may be angry about the nondonor's refusal to donate. In response to these feelings, nondonors may avoid contact with the potential recipient, which may only heighten the conflict within the family. The refusal to donate does not always decrease family cohesiveness (Abram & Buchanan, 1976), especially when requests for donation, refusals, and indecisions were handled through indirect communication (Simmons & Klein, 1972; Simmons, Klein, & Simmons, 1977). Nondonors may later be reintegrated into the family by providing financial assistance, child care, or other forms of support (Simmons, Klein, & Simmons, 1977).

CLINICAL IMPLICATIONS

The ability of the family to cope with the considerable stress of kidney transplantation has a significant impact on the psychological, social, and vocational adjustment of the patient. Family therapists can play a vital role in the preoperative assessment of patients and their families, as well as in the postoperative treatment of any family problems that develop.

As part of the preoperative assessment, the family therapist should explain to the family the psychosocial risks and benefits of surgery, including the changes that may occur in the family as the patient becomes healthy. In addition, the therapist should identify current family dysfunction and potential problems in adaptation. This psychosocial assessment should take place as soon as the patient is considered a candidate for transplantation, before perceptions are significantly influenced by the stress of the procedure. It should encompass the following topics:

1. history of stress and coping

   - How did the patient and family cope with stress prior to the onset of renal failure?
   - Was the patient on dialysis? If so, what was the patient's relationship with the dialysis staff? How did the family cope with dialysis?
   - How compliant has the patient been with medical treatments?

2. psychological status

   - What was the patient's premorbid personality?
   - Does the patient, or any other family member, demonstrate signs of depression, guilt, fear, denial, or anxiety to a degree that may hinder compliance with treatment?

- Does the patient appear to have a self-destructive potential?
- What motivates the patient to live?
- What does the transplant mean to the patient and family?
- Is the donor emotionally stable and intellectually capable of understanding the risks and benefits associated with the surgery?

3. family structure and stability

- What are the strengths within the family?
- Is there a history of family dysfunction?
- How flexible are roles within the family?
- To what degree do family members demonstrate social skills, including the ability to communicate directly with one another?
- What is the financial status of the family?
- What sources of support do family members have outside the family?
- How accepted does the patient feel by his/her spouse and family?
- To what degree is sexual frustration a concern for the patient or his/her spouse?
- How well do the patient and family appear to be managing the decision-making process surrounding the donor search?
- Are potential donors being pressured by the family?
- Is there a conflict between the donor's family of origin and family of procreation?
- What is the current frequency and type of contact among family members?
- Are there conflicts between the donor and the recipient?

There may be much more time and flexibility to prepare those who anticipate a transplant from a living relative than to prepare those who are on 24-hour call, waiting for a cadaver donor.

Particular care should be taken to prepare those who have been shown to be at high risk for poor adaptation. In some cases, such as those in which there is significant family dysfunction, the family therapist should recommend the postponement of surgery. Several options may then be presented to the patient family: (1) brief, ventilative, supportive therapy in which family members can discuss their fears and concerns; (2) family therapy to work on dysfunctions that may affect the outcome of surgery; and/or (3) assistance in obtaining social support from friends and the community.

Patients and their families may experience the greatest amount of stress soon after surgery, when the risk of kidney rejection is greatest and the patient's dosage of steroid medication is highest. This is a critical time for further psychosocial assessment:

- What changes have occurred in the family structure as a result of the transplant?
- Has the patient developed postoperative complications or experienced side-effects from the immunosuppressive drugs?
- How are the patient and family reacting to these? Do they view them as treatable?
- How is the patient accepting a body part (the kidney) from another individual?
- To what degree do the patient and family have a sense of control over nontreatment aspects of their life?
- Have there been barriers in the vocational rehabilitation of the patient?
- What is the patient's current relationship with the donor and other family members?
- What support systems have the patient and family established outside the family?

Follow-up assessment and treatment, if necessary, should continue periodically to ensure adjustment of the patient and the family after the patient's discharge from the hospital and during any medical complications that develop.

Kidney transplantation can be a challenging and rewarding process for the recipient and family, as well as for the staff involved in their care. For the family therapist, it provides an opportunity to participate in a biopsychosocial model of patient care.

REFERENCES

Abram, H.S., & Buchanan, D.C. (1976). The gift of life: A review of the psychological aspects of kidney transplantation. *International Journal of Psychiatry in Medicine, 7*(2), 153–164.

Basch, S.H. (1973). The intrapsychic integration of a new organ: A clinical study of kidney transplantation. *Psychoanalytic Quarterly, 42*(3), 364–384.

Buchanan, D.C. (1975). Group therapy for kidney transplant patients. *International Journal of Psychiatry in Medicine, 6*(4), 523–531.

Cain, L.P., & Staver, N. (1976). Helping children adapt to parental illness. *Social Casework, 57* No. 9, 575–580.

Carosella, J. (1984). Picking up the pieces: The unsuccessful kidney transplant. *Health and Social Work, 9* No. 2, 142–152.

Cramond, W.A. (1971). Renal transplantations: Experiences with recipients and donors. *Seminars in Psychiatry, 3*(1), 116–132.

Devins, G.M., Binik, Y.M., Hollomby, D.J., Barre, P.E., & Guttman, R.D. (1981). Helplessness and depression in end-stage renal disease. *Journal of Abnormal Psychology, 90*(6), 531–545.

Eisendrath, R.M. (1976). Adaptation to renal transplantation. In J.G. Howells (Ed.), Modern perspectives in the psychiatric aspects of surgery. New York: Brunner/Mazel.

Fellner, C.H. (1971). Selection of living kidney donors and the problem of informed consent. *Seminars in Psychiatry, 3*(1), 79–85.

Fielding, J.M. (1972). Psychiatric aspects of renal homo-transplantation. *Australian and New Zealand Journal of Psychiatry, 6*(57), 57–60.

Fife, B.L. (1985). A model for depicting the adaptation of families to medical crises: An analysis of role integration. *Image: The Journal of Nursing Scholarship, 17*(4), 108–112.

Freyberger, H. (1980). Renal transplant unit. *Advances in Psychosomatic Medicine, 10*, 151–177.

Glass, L., & Hickerson, M. (1976). Dialysis and transplantation: A mother's group. *Social Work in Health Care, 1*(3), 287–296.

Higgerson, A.B., & Bulechek, G.M. (1982). A descriptive study concerning the psychosocial dimensions of living related kidney donation. *American Association of Nephrology Nurses and Technicians, 9*(6), 27–31.

Kemph, J.P. (1966). Renal failure, artificial kidney and kidney transplant. *American Journal of Psychiatry, 122*, 1270–1274.

Knight, J.A. (1980). The liaison psychiatrist in kidney transplantation. *International Journal of Psychiatry in Medicine, 10*(3), 221–233.

Lohr, L. (1981). My kidney transplant. . . with a little help from my friends. *American Association of Nephrology Nurses and Technicians, 8*, 56–58.

McCubbin, H., McCubbin, M., Patterson, J., Cauble, A., Wilson, L., & Warwick, W. (1983). Coping health inventory for parents: An assessment of parental coping patterns in care of chronically ill child. *Journal of Marriage and the Family, 45*(2), 359–370.

Musial, E.M. (1980). An unsung hero—The living related kidney donor. *Nephrology Nurse, 2*(1), 21–62.

Payne, G.M., & Harrison, B. (1984). Reducing stress in renal patients and their families: A nurse-managed patient support group. *Journal of Nephrology Nursing, 1*(3), 138–140.

Sampson, T.F. (1975). The child in renal failure: Emotional impact of treatment on the child and his family. *Journal of the American Academy of Child Psychiatry, 14*(3), 462–476.

Schumann, D. (1974). The renal donor. *American Journal of Nursing, 74*(1), 105–110.

Simmons, R.G., Hickey, K., Kjellstrand, C.M., & Simmons, R.L. (1971). Donors and non-donors: The role of the family and the physician in kidney transplantation. *Seminars in Psychiatry, 3*(1), 102–115.

Simmons, R.G., & Klein, S.D. (1972). Family noncommunication: The search for kidney donors. *American Journal of Psychiatry, 129*(6), 687–692.

Simmons, R.G., Klein, S.D., & Simmons, R.L. (1977). *Gift of life: The social and psychological impact of organ transplantation.* New York: John Wiley & Sons.

Stewart, R.S. (1983). Psychiatric issues in renal dialysis and transplantation. *Hospital and Community Psychiatry, 34*(7), 623–628.

Topor, M.A. (1981). Renal transplantation in children. *American Association of Nephrology Nurses and Technicians, 8*(1), 14–18.

Wenzl, J.E. (1975). Preparation of patient and family for renal transplantation from a related donor. *Journal of Clinical Child Psychology, 4*(3), 41–43.

3. Families and Chronic Illness

Alberta Koch-Hattem, PhD
Director of Behavioral Medicine
University of North Carolina
Chapel Hill, North Carolina

T he prevalence of chronic illnesses has increased in recent years, apparently because medical advances have reduced the risk of infectious diseases and saved the lives of many who might in the past have died as a result of birth trauma or accident (Craig & Edwards, 1983; Rae-Grant, 1985; Thomas, 1984). Therefore, more families are faced with the care of chronically ill members. In addition, the effective control of chronic mental illnesses by psychotropic medications and the de-institutionalization of both the chronically mentally ill and the mentally retarded have allowed patients who might previously have been institutionalized to live with their families.

Chronic illnesses have been defined as conditions that cause anatomical or physiological changes; they are characterized by alternating periods of stability and crisis, alterations in life style and need for care, low probability of improvement, and either the possibility or the certainty of a decreased life span. Families of chronically ill patients must adapt to the patient's treatment, to the uncertainties of crises and death, to the changes in the patient's functioning and appearance, and to the increased requirements for care. The task of adapting to the illness varies with the nature of the illness and its treatment, the extent to which it disables or threatens the life of the patient, the patient's role(s) in the family, the family's prior experience and attitudes about illness, and the family's developmental stage. A given family's success in adapting to a chronic illness depends on its previous level of functioning, its resources, the meanings it attaches to the illness and the resulting changes in the patient and family, and its flexibility in the face of change (Anderson, 1981; Craig & Edwards, 1983; Drotar & Crawford, 1985; Glenn, 1982; Krulick, 1980; Rae-Grant, 1985; Sabbeth, 1984; Thomas, 1984; Venters, 1981).

The diagnosis of a chronic illness generally produces some form of crisis or disorganization in the family. In assessing the extent and outcome of the crisis, it is useful to examine the stressful events that are already confronting the family, the meaning that the family ascribes to the illness, and the family's resources for managing these stressors and those that will arise during the course of the chronic illness and its treatment (Hill, 1949, 1958; Koch, 1985a; McCubbin & Patterson, 1983).

STRESS AND THE ONSET OF CHRONIC ILLNESS

Every family experiences life cycle stressors associated with transitions in the development of the family as a whole and in the development of each family member. A chronic illness adds new stressors to those already present in the family. These new stressors include the financial burden of medical treatment and the management of the patient at home. When the patient is an adult, the financial burden may extend to lost income. When the patient is a child, management may require a parent to take time away from work or from the care of the patient's siblings to accompany the patient to clinic appointments or remain with the patient overnight in the hospital.

Little research has been undertaken to demonstrate the impact of stressors other than those associated with the illness on family adaptation to chronic illnesses. Patterson and McCubbin (1983) have found a relationship between the number of family stressors and changes in pulmonary functioning in children with cystic fibrosis, however. In addition, laboratory research has indicated that increased stress in marital communication correlates with an increased concentration of free fatty acids in children with diabetic acidosis (Minuchin, Rosman, & Baker, 1978). Finally, mental health researchers have demonstrated a relationship between an increase in family stressors and both depression in an ambulatory family practice population and adjustment to marital dissolution (Koch-Hattem, Alexander, et al., in preparation; Plummer & Koch-Hattem, in press).

DEFINITION OF THE STRESSOR

The particular meanings that family members ascribe to a chronic illness vary with the family's paradigm (i.e., view of the world), the family's beliefs about health and illness, and the family members' previous experiences with illness (Anderson, 1981; Glenn, 1982; Krulick, 1980; Reiss, 1981; Sargent,

1983; Thomas, 1984; Turk & Kerns, 1985; Venters, 1981). Does the family view the world as relatively safe, predictable, and susceptible to some degree of control? Does the family believe that illness is the result of an individual's poor health habits or personal weakness? Is sickness associated with dependence, incompetence, or helplessness? How effectively has the family coped with previous illnesses?

The meaning of the illness to the family may also be influenced by members' perceptions of the meaning of the illness to the physician. Family members may attempt to gauge the seriousness of the illness by the physician's presentation of it. For example, the physician may present the diagnosis, treatment plan, and prognosis in a matter-of-fact manner in an attempt to minimize the emotional responses of the patient and the family, and to keep the focus on treatment protocols. Family members may interpret this type of presentation as an indication that the physician does not care about them and is, therefore, not providing the best medical care. Alternately, they may conclude that the illness is so serious that the physician has no hope for the patient or that the illness is not sufficiently serious to merit concern.

Some theorists have postulated that there is a linkage between the meaning that the family ascribes to a stressor, such as a chronic illness, and the family's adaptation to it (Hill, 1949, 1958; McCubbin & Patterson, 1983). Family stress and mental health researchers have indeed demonstrated a relationship between meaning, in terms of the perceived severity of a stressor, and the effectiveness of family adaptation to it (Koch-Hattem, Alexander, et al., in preparation; McCubbin et al., 1980; Plummer & Koch-Hattem, in press). When families view the world as relatively safe, predictable, and susceptible to control and when they view the course of illness as a process on which family efforts can have a positive influence, adaptation to the chronic illness may be more effective (Anderson, 1981; Glenn, 1982; Koch, 1985a; Krulick, 1980; McCubbin & Patterson, 1983; Reiss, 1981; Sargent, 1983; Thomas, 1984; Turk & Kerns, 1985; Venters, 1981).

The meaning of the chronic illness to family members also has implications for compliance with treatment and, thus, prognosis (Anderson, 1981; Koch, 1985a). While denial of the seriousness of a chronic illness may be beneficial in specific contexts for limited time periods, it is detrimental to the patient's health to minimize the severity of an illness, especially one that requires self-care for effective control (Craig & Edwards, 1983).

RESOURCES FOR COPING

There are four categories of potential resources for managing a chronic illness and the other stressors that affect the family: (1)financial, (2) social, (3) personal, and (4) mental health.

Financial Resources

Without a health insurance or health maintenance policy that will cover the cost of treating the chronic illness, a family with a chronically ill member may be forced to deplete savings; accumulate large debts; move to less expensive housing, with the attendant disruption of neighborhood and school relationships; and otherwise lower its standard of living. A related financial resource is the flexibility of adult family members' work schedules. Some family members may lose income or even their jobs if they take time away from work when the patient needs additional care or is in the hospital. It may be necessary for the secondary, or even primary, wage earner to take a leave of absence or quit a job to care for the patient—at a time when the income is essential to maintain the family's life style.

Finally, potential wage earners in the family may be affected by a chronic illness. Goldman, Cohn, and Longnecker (1980–1981) described a family in which a young adult child delayed college plans in order to assist the family financially when the father was disabled by diabetes.

Social Resources

If the patient is a child and neither parent can take time from work, someone else must be available to take the child to the doctor and to administer medications. Similarly, someone must be available to act as a surrogate parent to the patient's healthy siblings so that their lives can continue as normally as possible. Families of chronically ill and handicapped children usually adapt more effectively to the illness or disability when they have social networks available to help them (Ferrari, 1984; Kazak & Marvin, 1984; Koch, 1985b; McCubbin et al., 1982; Shapiro, 1983; Venters, 1981). A family's social network may include grandparents, uncles and aunts, neighbors, friends, co-workers, members of the family's church or synagogue, parents of the healthy siblings' friends, and trusted babysitters or other child care workers. Healthy siblings may also turn to their teachers for emotional support.

If the chronically ill patient is an adult, social resources may include a member of the extended family or a friend who is willing to assume some of the patient's roles within the family. The family may have fewer social resources if the chronically ill member is an adult, however, as adults generally maintain the family's social network. When the adult family member who has been delegated the responsibility for maintaining the family's social network becomes chronically ill, therefore, the family's social resources may be even more depleted.

Personal Resources

Turk and Kerns (1985) have argued that family systems theorists tend to overlook the needs and resources of individual family members. Systems theory, however, requires researchers and practitioners to focus on multiple levels of the family system: the individual member subsystems; the marital, parental, parent-child, and sibling subsystems; the nuclear family; the extended family; and the family-community systems, including physicians and therapists (Doherty & Baird, 1983; Kantor & Lehr, 1975; Koch & Ingram, 1985; Sabbeth, 1984; Williamson, 1985). The issue then becomes one of focus.

The personal resources that an individual may use to manage the demands of a chronic illness in a family member include self-esteem, mental health (i.e., freedom from psychopathology), a sense of physical and emotional well-being, intelligence, education, and the belief that every individual can influence events (Anderson, 1981; Craig & Edwards, 1983; Drotar & Crawford, 1985; Glenn, 1982; Rae-Grant, 1985; Sabbeth, 1984; Sargent, 1983; Thomas, 1984; Venters, 1981). Orr, Weller, Satterwhite, and Pless (1984) noted that an individual's perceived freedom from organic health problems provides a global index of that individual's emotional well-being and high self-esteem. Conversely, perceptions of health problems are associated with anxiety, depression, and low self-esteem.

With respect to mental health, Lansky (1981), as well as Koch and Ingram (1985), argued that self-destructive behaviors indicative of psychopathology must be changed before marital or family therapy can be successful. Clinical experience also indicates that the self-absorption inherent in depression, anxiety, and personality disorders precludes family work until some symptom relief occurs. It may be assumed that a family member with any of these difficulties is not maximally available to participate in family efforts to cope with a chronic illness.

It is difficult to determine the differential impact of adult and child chronic illness on the family's personal resources. Although work has been done on depression and self-esteem in both chronically ill children and chronically ill adults, it has not been documented whether chronically ill adults are more likely to experience depression and reduced self-esteem than are chronically ill children. Adult and child conceptualizations of health, illness, and death differ, consistent with developmental differences.

Although Rinaldi (1985) noted that the use of psychotherapy as an adjunct improves the effectiveness of medical treatment, the relationship between family members' mental health and their adaptation to chronic illness has not been empirically examined. Moreover, no specific definition of mental health has been established. Personal resources, such as the level of father's education and the presence of a mother who does not work outside the home, have been linked to family adaptation to cystic fibrosis, however, as indicated by compliance with treatment (Patterson, 1985).

Mental Health Resources

Sometimes labeled family structural resources, mental health resources have two components: family flexibility and family rules concerning the management of affect.

Flexibility. The demands of a chronic illness in a family member may necessitate changes in family roles, routines, and boundaries (Koch, 1985a; Sargent, 1983). These demands for change are additional stressors to which the family must adapt, and lack of family flexibility may engender yet more stressors (McCubbin & Patterson, 1983).

Virtually every conceptualization of family adaptation to any stressful event includes some consideration of family flexibility (Burr, 1973; Hansen & Johnson, 1979; Hill, 1949, 1958; Kantor, 1980; Koch, 1985a; McCubbin & Patterson, 1983; Olson, Sprenkle, & Russell, 1979; Pratt, 1976). Research based on family stress theory has demonstrated a relationship between role flexibility in assuming daily tasks, particularly those tasks that change after the onset of a stressful event, and effective adaptation to the stressor (Koch, 1985b; Koch-Hattem, Alexander, et al., in preparation; McCubbin et al., 1980; McCubbin et al., 1982; McCubbin & Patterson, 1982; Patterson & McCubbin, 1983). Although much of this research has focused on flexibility in regard to routine tasks, Kantor (1980), and Kantor and Lehr (1975), demonstrated that flexibility in communication may be associated with both the mental health of family members and family adaptation to life cycle stressors. Koch (1985b) found that families in which members share the responsibility of providing one another with emotional support appear to adapt more effectively to childhood cancer than do those in which emotional care-giving is assigned to a single member; Koch also found that role flexibility among healthy siblings may be associated with what their parents refer to as "maturity beyond their years."

Olson and his associates (1979) described a circumplex model of family adaptation in which flexibility along two dimensions—adaptability and cohesion—characterize effective adaptation. They defined adaptability as the extent to which family members are flexible in their role taking; end points of this continuum are chaotic (i.e., overly flexible) and rigid (i.e., inflexible). They defined cohesion as the closeness-distance component of family relationships; end points are enmeshed (i.e., closeness that precludes flexible boundaries among family members) and disengaged (i.e., boundaries that are so inflexible that they cannot be crossed). Families that fall toward the midpoints of both dimensions may adapt more effectively to stress (Olson, McCubbin, & Lavee, 1984).

Hansen and Johnson (1979), and McCubbin and Patterson (1983), described flexibility of communication in terms of negotiation of family roles and rules.

> The parents of a leukemic child whose disease had been in a stable remission for several years continued to worry about their daughter's prognosis. The mother, on the one hand, attempted to engage the father in a discussion of her concerns. The father, on the other hand, coped with his fears by avoiding any discussion of them. The more the wife talked about the child's cancer, the more the husband withdrew from her.

Sabbeth (1984) argued that such complementarity of communication roles may be adaptive; however, an ability to negotiate alternative ways to communicate about their daughter's cancer would have demonstrated flexible communication.

A final characteristic of family flexibility as a mental health resource is the maintenance of a balance between member and family needs. Despite the demands of patient care, the family that adapts effectively to the chronic illness continues to attend to the autonomy and developmental needs of all family members (Grieco & Kopel, 1983; Hauser, Jacobson, Wertlieb, Brink, & Wentworth, 1985; Kantor & Lehr, 1975; Napier & Whitaker, 1978; Racy, 1983; Venters, 1981).

Management of Affect. Family rules may be conceptualized as the structure through which family members negotiate adaptive changes in the presence of chronic stressors (McCubbin & Patterson, 1983). When a chronic illness is diagnosed, family members experience a variety of feelings about the illness, the patient, the family, and their own health: sadness, irritation, resentment, anger, anxiety, depression, worry about the patient, fear of death, jealousy, guilt, and inadequacy. When the illness is inherited, these feelings may be exacerbated. In addition, family members must mourn the loss of the patient and the family as they were and might have been. Finally, when the chronically ill or disabled family member is a child, the parents must mourn the loss of their dreams for their child (Comaroff & Maguire, 1981; Farkas, 1980; Gottschalk, 1983; Koch, 1985b; Koch-Hattem, 1986; Kramer, 1981; Peck, 1979; Racy, 1983; Shapiro, 1983).

In order to cope effectively with the chronic illness, family members must find ways of managing these feelings. Families appear either to rely on previous family rules or to develop new rules to permit or prohibit members' expression of these feelings (Broderick & Smith, 1979). When a family prohibits the expression of affect, family members must find alternate ways to cope with these feelings. Some family members involve themselves in projects, others exercise, and still others withdraw to places where they can be alone. Some family members may become aggressive outside the family, engage in self-destructive behaviors, or lie awake at night worrying about the patient. There is an inverse relationship between a family's prohibition of emotional expression and an effective adaptation to chronic illness (Koch, 1983, 1985a, 1985b; Koch-Hattem, Hattem, & Plummer, in preparation).

OUTCOME OF ADAPTATION

According to Hill (1949, 1958), the outcome of family adaptation to stressors can be either an effective or ineffective reorganization of the family. McCubbin and Patterson (1983) viewed adaptation as a continuum, ranging from maladaptation to bonadaptation, and described outcome as a process that follows the initial crisis and includes adaptation to the stressors engendered by it. In medical practice, illness outcome is the improvement, deterioration, or maintenance of the patient's condition relative to the physician's expectations. By definition, a chronic illness is likely either to worsen or remain the same. Thus, a positive outcome for a chronic illness can be exemplified by a hypertensive patient's return to work and family responsibilities within the limits of his or her physical condition following a myocardial infarction, as well as controlled blood pressure and normal electrocardiograph readings. A negative outcome can be exemplified by the patient's withdrawal from work and family responsibilities, irrespective of his or her ability to perform them, or by unexplained periods in which the patient's blood pressure cannot be controlled despite compliance with the treatment protocol.

The details of the outcome of family adaptation to chronic illnesses have not been well specified in the literature. Most of the available literature has focused on the outcome of family adaptation to chronic childhood illness; however, the body of literature on the impact of chronic illness on an adult patient's spouse and the impact of chronically ill adults and children on the family as a whole is growing. Researchers have identified both negative and positive outcomes, ranging from symptoms of organic and mental distress in the patient and other family member(s), marital dissolution, and noncompliance with treatment regimens to increases in family cohesion, more emotional freedom in communication, and compliance with treatment regimens (Boss, 1985; Ferrari, 1984; Goldman et al., 1980–1981; Koch, 1985b; Patterson, 1985; Racy, 1983; Rowat & Knafl, 1985; Sabbeth, 1984; Turk & Kerns, 1985).

The outcomes of family adaptation to chronic illness may occur on the family system level, the marital subsystem level, and the individual subsystem level (Koch, 1985a; Sabbeth, 1984). In some families, for example, the care of a chronically ill grandparent increases family cohesion, marital intimacy, and individual differentiation and well-being. In other families, however, it is associated with family members' perception of each other as more remote and inaccessible, increased marital conflict over the grandparent's care, and somatic symptoms in the person primarily responsible for that care. Furthermore, there are both physical and mental health outcomes. Somatic complaints from the person primarily responsible for the aging parent's care are medically real, but may originate in decreased mental health. Family therapists' interventions may focus on the mental health outcomes of family adaptation, while health care providers may aim their interventions at the physical health outcomes of this process.

The scant literature on the impact of chronic illness on the family as a whole has focused on enmeshment as a dysfunctional coping strategy (Sargent, 1983, Swanson & Maruta, 1980; Turk & Kerns, 1985). It is not clear from this literature, however, whether a positive feedback loop between enmeshment and the patient's health develops, whether enmeshment predisposes to chronic illness, or whether chronic illness predisposes to enmeshment. Although circular causality and focus on the present are hallmarks of family therapy, punctuating observation of the family system at the onset of an event, such as the diagnosis of a chronic illness, may be useful. For example, if it could be demonstrated that enmeshment predisposes to chronic illness, physicians may wish to screen families routinely for enmeshment and intervene as a pro- phylactic measure. On the other hand, if chronic illness predisposes to enmesh- ment, early treatment of chronic illness may include a family therapy component aimed at preventing the development of an enmeshed family structure. From a more systemic perspective, the ability of family therapists to punctuate their observations in terms of the onset of the chronic illness may help them to discriminate between dysfunctional coping with the illness and long-term dysfunctional patterns within the family. Intervention designed to alter dysfunctional coping in families that were previously functional may be both more brief and more simple than intervention designed to alter dysfunc- tional patterns that have been exacerbated by the illness.

CASE EXAMPLE

Bob and Susan Smith-Jones, a couple in their early 40s, lived in an upper middle class suburb of a southeastern city. Both worked outside the home, and both were committed to their careers.

Their 14-year-old daughter, Jane, had recently entered high school and was demanding more autonomy in managing her social activities and her schedule for homework and chores. Bob and Susan believed that Jane was still too young to make such decisions and needed to spend more time with the family. As part of their effort to change Jane's behavior, Bob delegated to Susan the responsibility for seeing that Jane does her homework every night. Although Susan said that she was usually too busy and blamed Jane for being irresponsible, she did not challenge Bob's refusal to help. Jane's grades dropped, from all As to Bs and Cs, and she was described as unpleasant to family members. Dick, Jane's 11-year-old brother, met the parents' definition of an exemplary child. His grades were all As, he had many friends, he was active in sports and Boy Scouts, and he was helpful and loving at home. The youngest child, 7-year-old Sally, did well in school, played well with her peers, and was pleasant and cooperative at home.

At the time that Jane's behavior was causing stress in the family, it was discovered that Sally had acute lymphocytic leukemia (ALL), the most common and effectively managed childhood cancer. Sally was hospitalized for 2 weeks while the pediatrician and pediatric oncologists arrived at the diagnosis and began treatment. During that time, Susan stayed at the hospital with Sally most nights, and Bob remained at home with Jane and Dick. When the disease was diagnosed, the medical team allowed the parents to vent their feelings and to ask whatever questions they wished. A follow-up visit with the medical team was scheduled for a month later, after the parents had had time to absorb the news and to begin to cope with it. The medical team offered to help the parents tell Sally and her siblings about the diagnosis (Gamstorp, 1980; Rae-Grant, 1985).

The treatment of Sally's leukemia required management of her medical regimen, including the administration of medication at home and in both outpatient and inpatient settings, frequent checkups, and possibly hospitalizations. Someone had to accompany Sally to her medical appointments, and her parents decided that Susan would stay with her whenever she was hospitalized. Sally experienced several side-effects of treatment: hair loss, weight gain, nausea, fatigue, missed school, and temporary inability to engage in chores, family activities, and social activities outside the home. Efforts to cope with the demands of Sally's illness created certain stressors in the family. For example, as Sally became the center of the family's activities and concerns, Dick attempted ineffectively to regain parental attention; he missed school and withdrew from friends in order to be with the patient and help his parents (Ferrari, 1984; Koch, 1985b; Koch-Hattem, 1986; Krulick, 1980).

Bob and Susan were concerned about the cost of Sally's treatments and the loss of Susan's income during periods when Sally needed special care. Bob's health insurance policy provided sufficient coverage to keep the cost of treating Sally's leukemia below $20,000, however. The joint income of Bob and Susan allowed the family to maintain its previous life style, but the savings that had been earmarked for the children's education were spent on Sally's medical care. As Jane had fantasized about gaining autonomy when she left home to attend college, she was the first to be affected by the depletion of the family's financial resources. She viewed the situation as further proof that her parents cared more for her siblings than for her, and she felt guilty for resenting the cost of Sally's treatments.

Susan's job provided enough flexibility that she could take time as needed to care for Sally; however, family routines changed in Susan's absence, particularly with respect to meal preparation, cleaning, laundry, and bedtime. Bob assumed some supervisory responsibility for these activities, but insisted that Jane undertake most of Susan's tasks during Sally's hospitalizations. Several of Susan's co-workers helped the family from time to time, and Susan was able to rely on her previous arrangements for the after-school activities of the older children.

While members of the Smith-Jones family had a number of friends, they generally did not discuss their feelings and problems with people outside the family. Jane was able to talk to Susan's sister, and Dick told a coach at school about Sally's illness. Susan and Bob, however, had always prided themselves on appearing happy and self-sufficient. People outside the family tended to assume that Susan and Bob had no problems and could cope with whatever happened to them. Because they wished to maintain this appearance, they declined to participate in a support group for parents of pediatric cancer patients and attempted to hide their distress from Sally's physicians (Sabbeth, 1984). Both relied on Susan's sister and mother for emotional support, however.

All the members of the Smith-Jones family were intelligent, and both Bob and Susan were highly educated. Moderate self-esteem, external locus of control, and anxiety around well-being were also characteristic of them, however. Susan had been treated for depression shortly after leaving her family of origin and had feared that she and/or Jane would become depressed or suicidal when Jane's behavior became a problem. She relayed this information tearfully, and Jane began to cry. It was thus apparent that Susan's reaction to her past reverberated through this family.

Bob, on the other hand, grew up in a chaotic family and prided himself on being organized, competent, and in control of every situation. He crossed the room to comfort first Susan and then Jane, his face and posture rigid.

The Smith-Jones family needed to develop flexibility in three areas: (1) boundaries, (2) routines, and (3) family roles. Even before Sally became ill, Jane's growth into adolescence required Bob and Susan to allow her more freedom in managing her time and engaging in extrafamilial activities. Similarly, as the family mourned the loss of Sally's health and possibly her future, a second shift in boundaries within the family could be expected to occur. As previously noted, primary responsibility for meal preparation had been delegated to Jane when Susan was unavailable because of Sally's illness; optimal adaptation might be achieved if the burden of Susan's tasks were redistributed more evenly throughout the nuclear family and the social network. Finally, the illness necessitated role flexibility in this family. Sally's role changed by virtue of her illness. When she suffered side-effects of treatment or when the illness was progressing, she was not able to participate in chores or family activities and sometimes could not even go to school. At these times, she required an inordinate amount of parental attention, and Susan was required to make additional compensations in her usual roles. Moreover, because prior parenting behaviors did not seem appropriate or feel comfortable to Susan and Bob when Sally was sick, they felt it necessary to increase their parenting repertoire (Krulick, 1980).

Sally's healthy siblings took over her chores when she was incapacitated, but Bob did not assume Susan's routine tasks when Sally's treatment made additional demands on her. The attention that Bob and Susan paid to the developmental and emotional needs of their healthy children was relatively unchanged; their focus on Sally did not preclude their other parenting activities.

Sally's parents and siblings reported that they were experiencing many of the feelings identified by researchers. Everyone agreed that they mostly kept these feelings to themselves or tried not to think about them. They also agreed that this was the best way to handle these feelings. When asked whether they had been comfortable when someone expressed feelings before Sally's leukemia was diagnosed, Bob smiled and said, "no;" Jane snorted; Dick shifted in his chair and looked at the floor; and Susan said through gritted teeth, "We get upset with each other, but we're not allowed to say anything."

Susan worried that Sally's illness could be attributed to her working outside the home, although she said she knew that was ridiculous. Although family members had had no prior experience with serious acute or chronic illness, they believed that Sally's illness was serious. Finally, they believed that, if the whole family worked together, they might be able to make a difference in Sally's recovery.

The Smith-Jones family's strategies for coping with Sally's illness and its treatment involved increased togetherness. They blocked Jane's fantasies of escape to college; placed greater demands on Susan to balance career with home and child care; defined Sally's illness as the priority for all family members; maintained a happy, self-sufficient facade; and placed more demands on Jane to spend time with the family, in part because "Who knows how much more time we all have together?" These coping strategies exacerbated the enmeshment of the family by impeding member differentiation. This enmeshment increased not only the unresolved conflict within the marital subsystem and the parent-child subsystem that included Jane, but also the potential for marital distress and adolescent misbehavior.

Jane's ineffective methods of asserting her autonomy increased; she failed algebra and befriended a group of whom her parents disapproved. As these negative behaviors escalated, the Smith-Jones family became a more likely candidate for family therapy. It is possible that family interventions provided by a family therapist or family physician involved in Sally's treatment could have prevented this deterioration in family and family member functioning.

INTERVENTION

As noted earlier, family therapy interventions for families of chronically ill patients must consider the way in which families functioned at the onset of the illness. Families may be placed in one of three categories. First, a family that has been flexible in adapting to other stressors; has successfully balanced affiliation with differentiation of members; has a range of financial, personal, social, and mental health resources at its disposal; and tends to assign realistic and manageable meanings to stressors is likely to make an effective adaptation to the chronic illness. Second, a family that was dysfunctional prior to the onset of the illness, as characterized by inflexibility in adapting to other stressors, enmeshment or disengagement, depleted resources, and a tendency either to deny or to catastrophize stressful events is unlikely to make an effective adaptation to the chronic illness. Third, a family that is minimally distressed at the time of the diagnosis becomes vulnerable to an ineffective adaptation, characterized by family dysfunction; the Smith-Jones family exemplifies this category of families. Assessment to place a particular family in one of these three categories is the first step in determining the nature of the appropriate intervention and the role of the family therapist.

Family stress theory can be used to guide interventions with all three types of families, although there is some conflict between the theory and the reality of clinical practice with families of chronically ill patients. There are limits in the practitioner's ability to (1) increase the family's financial and social resources following the diagnosis of a chronic illness and (2) change its history of adaptation to stressors. For example, family therapists are not usually trained to provide financial counseling. Furthermore, it is unrealistic to expect that family members would make the kind of significant life style change necessary to increase the family's financial resources while the family is faced with the expense of a chronic illness. Similarly, it is unlikely that a family with a restricted social network could muster the time and energy to expand that network when faced with a chronic illness, particularly if the illness is visible or otherwise stigmatized. Finally, only the present and future are susceptible to change.

Therapists can best serve families that have a pattern of effective adaptation to stressors by engaging them in preventive interventions. Such interventions are aimed at maintaining the family's strengths in the presence of the additional stressors associated with the chronic illness. When a family has a history of ineffective adaptation to stressors, the additional stressors associated with the chronic illness may be secondary to the family dysfunction. The family therapist may conceptualize the family's presumably ineffective adaptation to the chronic illness as yet another example of the need for family intervention. For these families, traditional family therapy interventions may be most effective (Koch, 1985a).

Family therapy interventions for families of chronically ill patients should be aimed at treating the dysfunction, with the goal of freeing these families to develop effective strategies for coping with the demands of the chronic illness.

Most authorities recommend the use of the structural family therapy model and its associated techniques for families that must adapt to a chronic illness (Drotar & Crawford, 1985; Frey, 1984; Sargent, 1983, 1985). Minuchin and his colleagues (1978) were very persuasive in describing the effectiveness of structural family therapy in treating chronic illnesses, particularly when acute episodes are associated with family distress, and case studies in which physicians used structural family therapy have clearly demonstrated the application of this model in clinical care. In family interventions aimed at weight control and other life style changes associated with the management of chronic illnesses, such as coronary artery disease, and at chronic pain, however, social learning theory and behavior modification techniques have been successful (Barbarin & Tirado, 1985; Block, Kremer, & Gayler, 1980; Doherty & Baird, 1983; Ewart, Burnett, & Taylor, 1983; Grieco & Kopel, 1983; Morse, 1983).

As families that were minimally dysfunctional at the onset of a chronic illness may be vulnerable to an ineffective adaptation to the chronic illness, or increased family dysfunction, both preventive and treatment interventions must be considered. Early, preventive interventions may strengthen the vulnerable family to the extent that it remains functional. Preventive interventions have the additional advantages of being less time-consuming, less costly, and less invasive. Family therapists, physicians, or an interdisciplinary team may begin with preventive interventions. The therapist or physician will recognize the point at which family dysfunction increases and it is necessary to shift to a family therapy treatment approach (Doherty & Baird, 1983; Koch, 1985a).

CONCLUSION

Family researchers and family therapists face major challenges in working with chronically ill patients and their families. Family assessments, interventions, and research are influenced by the interests of health care providers, the demands of health care settings, health care policy, and research funding. These economic, political, and service systems impinge on the family and influence its adaptation to chronic illness (Doherty & Baird, 1983; Grose & Goodrich, 1985; Sabbeth, 1984; Williamson, 1985). The impact of these larger systems on the functioning of families and those who observe and treat them cannot easily be ignored.

REFERENCES

Anderson, J.M. (1981). The social construction of illness experience: Families with a chronically ill child. *Journal of Advanced Nursing, 6,* 427–434.

Barbarin, O., & Tirado, M. (1985). Enmeshment, family processes, and successful treatment of obesity. *Family Relations, 34,* 115–121.

Block, A.R., Kremer, E.F., & Gayler, M. (1980). Behavioral treatment of chronic pain: The spouse as a discriminative cue for pain behavior. *Pain, 9,* 243–252.

Boss, P. (1985). Family stress: Perception and context. In M.B. Sussman & S. Steinmetz (Eds.), *Handbook on marriage and the family.* New York: Plenum Press.

Broderick, C., & Smith, J. (1979). The general systems approach to the family. In W.R. Burr, R. Hill, F.I. Nye, & I.L. Reiss (Eds.), *Contemporary theories about the family (Vol. 2).* New York: Free Press.

Burr, W.R. (1973). *Theory construction and the sociology of the family.* New York: John Wiley & Sons.

Comaroff, J., & Maguire, P. (1981). Ambiguity and the search for meaning: Childhood leukemia in the modern clinical context. *Social Science and Medicine, 15B,* 115–123.

Craig, H.M., & Edwards, J.E. (1983). Adaptation in chronic illness: An eclectic model for nurses. *Journal of Advanced Nursing, 8,* 397–404.

Doherty, W., & Baird, M. (1983). *Family therapy and family medicine: Toward the primary care of families.* New York: Guilford Press.

Drotar, D., & Crawford, P. (1985). Psychological adaptation of siblings of chronically ill children: Research and practice implications. *Journal of Developmental Behavioral Pediatrics, 6,* 355–362.

Ewart, C.K., Burnett, K.F., & Taylor, C.B. (1983). Communication behaviors that affect blood pressure: An A-B-A-B analysis of marital interaction. *Behavior Modification, 7,* 331–344.

Farkas, S.W. (1980). Impact of chronic illness on the patient's spouse. *Health and Social Work, 5,* 39–46.

Ferrari, M. (1984). Chronic illness: Psychosocial effects on siblings. *Journal of Child Psychology and Psychiatry, 25,* 459–476.

Frey, J., III. (1984). A family/systems approach to illness-maintaining behaviors in chronically ill adolescents. *Family Process, 23,* 251–260.

Gamstorp, I. (1980). The chronically ill, handicapped, dying child and his family: Need for total care and support. *Brain Development, 2,* 127–132.

Glenn, M.L. (1982). Family illness rituals. *Journal of Family Practice, 14,* 950–954.

Goldman, R.H., Cohn, G.L., & Longnecker, R.E. (1980–1981). The family and home hemo-dialysis: Adolescents' reactions to a father on home dialysis. *International Journal of Psychiatry and Medicine, 10,* 235–254.

Gottschalk, L.A. (1983). *Measurement of mood, affect, and anxiety in cancer patients.* Paper presented at the meeting of the American Cancer Society.

Grieco, A.L., & Kopel, K.F. (1983). Self-help and self-care in chronic illness. *Southern Medical Journal, 76,* 1128–1130.

Grose, N., & Goodrich, T.J. (1985). Chronicity and the physician. *Family Systems Medicine, 3,* 190–196.

Hansen, D.A., & Johnson, V.A. (1979). Rethinking family stress theory: Definitional aspects. In W.R. Burr, R. Hill, F.I. Nye, & I.L. Reiss (Eds.), *Contemporary theories about the family (Vol. 2).* New York: Free Press.

Hauser, S., Jacobson, A., Wertlieb, D., Brink, S., & Wentworth, S. (1985). The contribution of family environment to perceived competence and illness adjustment in diabetic and acutely ill adolescents. *Family Relations, 34,* 99–108.

Hill, R. (1949). *Families under stress.* New York: Harper & Row.

Hill, R. (1958). Generic features of families under stress. *Social Casework, 49,* 139–150.

Kantor, D. (1980). Critical identity image: A concept linking individual, couple, and family development. In J.K. Pearce & L.J. Friedman (Eds.), *Family therapy: Combining psychodynamic and family systems approaches*. New York: Grune & Stratton.

Kantor, D., & Lehr, W. (1975). *Inside the family: Toward a theory of family process*. New York: Harper & Row.

Kazak, A.E., & Marvin, R.S. (1984). Differences, difficulties, and adaptation: Stress and social networks in families with a handicapped child. *Family Relations, 33*, 67–77.

Koch, A. (1983). Family adaptation to medical stressors. *Family Systems Medicine, 1*, 78–87.

Koch, A. (1985a). A strategy for prevention: Role flexibility and affective reactivity as factors in family coping. *Family Systems Medicine, 3*, 70–81.

Koch, A. (1985b). "If only it could be me." The families of pediatric cancer patients. *Family Relations, 34*, 63–70.

Koch, A., & Ingram, T. (1985). The treatment of borderline personality disorder within a distressed relationship. *Journal of Marital and Family Therapy, 11*, 373–380.

Koch-Hattem, A. (1986). Siblings' experience of pediatric cancer. *Health and Social Work, 11*, 107–117.

Koch-Hattem, A., Alexander, M., Berolzheimer, N., Marshall, W., Olson, R., Thrower, S., Johnson, W., & Johnson, R. (in preparation). Family stress, coping, and depression. Unpublished manuscript.

Koch-Hattem, A., Hattem, D., & Plummer, L. (in preparation). The role of mental health resources in explaining family adaptation to stress. Unpublished manuscript.

Kramer, R. (1981). Living with childhood cancer: Healthy siblings' perspectives. *Issues in Comprehensive Pediatric Nursing, 5*, 155–165.

Krulick, T. (1980). Successful normalizing tactics of parents of chronically ill children. *Journal of Advanced Nursing, 5*, 573–578.

Lansky, M.R. (1981). Major psychopathology and the family. In M.R. Lansky (Ed.), *Family therapy and major psychopathology*. New York: Grune & Stratton.

McCubbin, H.I., Joy, C.B., Cauble, A.E., Comeau, J.K., Patterson, J.M., & Needle, R.H. (1980). Family stress and coping: A decade review. *Journal of Marriage and the Family, 42*, 855–871.

McCubbin, H.I., Nevin, R.S., Cauble, A.E., Larsen, A., Comeau, J.K., & Patterson, J.M. (1982). Family coping with chronic illness: The case of cerebral palsy. In H.I. McCubbin, A.E. Cauble, & J.M. Patterson (Eds.), *Family stress, coping, and social support*. Springfield, IL: Charles C Thomas.

McCubbin, H.I., & Patterson, J.M. (1982). Family adaptation to crises. In H.I. McCubbin, A.E. Cauble, & J.M. Patterson (Eds.), *Family stress, coping, and social support*. Springfield, IL: Charles C Thomas.

McCubbin, H.I., & Patterson, J.M. (1983). The family stress process: The double ABCX model of adjustment and adaptation. In H.I. McCubbin, M.B. Sussman, J.M. Patterson (Eds.), *Social stress and the family*. New York: Haworth Press.

Minuchin, S., Rosman, B.L., & Baker, L. (1978). *Psychosomatic families: Anorexia nervosa in context*. Cambridge, MA: Harvard University Press.

Morse, R.H. (1983). Chronic pain review: A family affair. *Journal of the Louisiana State Medical Society, 135*, 47–51.

Napier, A.Y., & Whitaker, C.A. (1978). *The family crucible*. New York: Harper & Row.

Olson, D., McCubbin, H.I., & Lavee, Y. (1984). *Integrating the circumplex model and FAAR model: Validity with 1000 families*. Paper presented to the National Council on Family Relations, San Francisco.

Olson, D.H., Sprenkle, D.H., & Russell, C.S. (1979). Circumplex model of marital and family systems: I. Cohesion and adaptability dimensions, family types, and clinical approaches. *Family Process, 18*, 3–28.

Orr, D.P., Weller, S.C., Satterwhite, B., & Pless, I.B. (1984). Psychosocial implications of chronic illness in adolescence. *Journal of Pediatrics, 104*, 152–157.

Patterson, J. (1985). Critical factors affecting family compliance with home treatment for children with cystic fibrosis. *Family Relations, 34*, 79–89.

Patterson, J.M., & McCubbin, H.I. (1983). The impact of family life events and changes on the health of a chronically ill child. *Family Relations, 32*, 255–264.

Peck, B. (1979). Effects of childhood cancer on long-term survivors and their families. *British Medicine Journal, 1*, 1327–1329.

Plummer, L., & Koch-Hattem A. (in press). Family stress and adjustment to divorce. *Family Relations*.

Pratt, L. (1976). *Family structure and effective health behavior: The energized family*. Boston, MA: Houghton-Mifflin.

Racy, J.C. (1983). The family and chronic disease. *Arizona Medicine, 40*, 854–857.

Rae-Grant, Q. (1985). Psychological problems in the medically ill child. *Psychiatric Clinics of North America, 8*, 653–663.

Reiss, D. (1981). *The family's construction of reality*. Cambridge, MA: Harvard University Press.

Rinaldi, R.C. (1985). Positive effects of psychosocial interventions in total health care: A review of the literature. *Family Systems Medicine, 3*, 417–426.

Rowat, K.M., & Knafl, K.A. (1985). Living with chronic pain. The spouse's perspective. *Pain, 23*, 259–271.

Sabbeth, B. (1984). Understanding the impact of chronic childhood illness on families. *Pediatric Clinics of North America, 31*, 47–57.

Sargent, J. (1983). The sick child. Family complications. *Journal of Developmental Behavioral Pediatrics, 4*, 50–56.

Sargent, J. (1985). Physician-family therapist collaboration: Children with medical problems. *Family Systems Medicine, 3*, 454–465.

Shapiro, J. (1983). Family reactions and coping strategies in response to the physically ill or handicapped child: A review. *Social Science and Medicine, 17*, 913–931.

Swanson, D.W., & Maruta, T. (1980). The family's viewpoint of chronic pain. *Pain, 8*, 163–166.

Thomas, R.B. (1984). Nursing assessment of childhood chronic conditions. *Issues in Comprehensive Pediatric Nursing, 7*, 165–176.

Turk, D.C., & Kerns, R.D. (1985). *Health, illness, and families: A life-span perspective*. New York: John Wiley & Sons.

Venters, M. (1981). Familial coping with chronic and severe childhood illness. *Social Science and Medicine, 15*, 289–297.

Williamson, P.S. (1985). Consequences for the family in chronic illness. *Journal of Family Practice, 21*, 23–32.

4. Families and Chronic Pain

Jeri Hepworth, PhD
Assistant Professor and
Director, Behavioral Science
Department of Family Medicine
University of Connecticut School of Medicine

F amily therapists have long been concerned with the interaction between individual physical symptoms and family responses (Weakland, 1977). Most therapists even have favorite stories that document the alleviation of some physical symptom by improvement in family interactional patterns or resolution of intergenerational conflicts (e.g., see Hepworth, 1987); however, many of these stories reflect physical symptoms that appeared only in the recent past or are already related to stress. There are also classic reports of a family process exacerbating chronic and life-threatening illnesses (Minuchin et al., 1975), but the treatment of these families is usually left to those who specialize in the treatment of the particular disorder. Many family therapists are not adequately informed about physical illness, and they are reluctant to become involved with clients who exhibit chronic or severe physical symptoms and their families.

This chapter will not provide complete information about the treatment of chronic pain. Therapists will not be the sole care providers for those with chronic pain. The complex relationships between medical, surgical, psycho-logical, and social treatments for pain usually require a multidisciplinary approach, an accepted tenet of chronic pain treatment (Sternbach, 1974). Family therapists should be familiar with the theoretical and clinical formula-tions about the relationship between chronic pain and family interactions, however, as well as with the role of family-oriented treatment within chronic pain treatment programs, so that they can work with other health care pro-viders in collaborative treatment relationships.

It has been estimated that 50 million (Roy, 1984) to 75 million (Kerns & Turk, 1984) Americans suffer from chronic physical pain. In a survey of 372 general population households, Crook, Rideout, and Browne (1984) found that 36% had one or more family members who had experienced pain in the preceding 2 weeks. Persistent pain, defined as "often bothered by pain," was reported by 24% of the sample. This finding is similar to Roy's (1984) report that as many as 35% of Americans may experience chronic pain. It is likely, therefore, that a significant proportion of any family therapist's caseload involves individuals and families who are directly or indirectly affected by chronic physical pain.

OVERVIEW OF PAIN MANAGEMENT

It is generally accepted that acute pain is a protective physiological mechanism that warns of impending or present tissue damage. Bergman and Werblun (1978) defined chronic pain as pain that continues for 6 months. They also noted that anxiety and depression become part of the individual's response to chronic pain. Most behavior associated with chronic pain has social and psychological meanings that are determined by the pain's duration and its interference with daily activities. As the pain stimulus becomes associated with rewarding social and psychological responses, the attention to the stimulus increases.

The interrelationship between psychological and physiological responses is the basis of most integrated treatment programs (Fordyce, 1976; Sternbach, 1974). In such programs, the distinction between psychosomatic and organic pain is dismissed as "simplistic" (Shanfield & Killingsworth, 1977) or as "pseudo-explanation" (Szasz, 1955). Patients are taught to use the psychological and learning processes that positively reinforce pain in ways that negatively reinforce symptoms and pain behavior. After it has been determined that surgical or medical treatment cannot eliminate the pain, treatment is designed to minimize pain behaviors and the resulting reinforcers, and to manage the pain in ways that maximize activity levels and social functioning.

Social learning theory or operant conditioning models of pain control are not the only methods of conceptualizing and treating pain behaviors. Medical treatments that focus on the individual patient may include surgery and/or medications, supplemented by physical therapy, corrective braces, acupuncture, group therapy, biofeedback, hypnosis, and other forms of relaxation training.

CHRONIC PAIN AND INDIVIDUAL PERSONALITY CHARACTERISTICS

With their individual psychiatric conceptualizations of pain behavior, several authors have described the personality characteristics likely to be found in patients with chronic pain. Perhaps the most widely cited personality profile is the "conversion V" profile of scores on the Minnesota Multiphasic Personality Inventory (MMPI), also known as the "neurotic triad." Patients with pain are reported to score high on three subscales of the MMPI: hypochondriasis, depression, and hysteria (Block & Boyer, 1984; Gentry, Shows, & Thomas, 1974; Greenhoot & Sternbach, 1977; Maruta & Osborne, 1978; Sternbach, 1974). Roberts and Reinhardt (1980) also reported that pain patients had elevated scores on these three MMPI subscales, but noted that the scores were significantly reduced after patients successfully completed a pain management program. They suggested that the elevated scores may reflect responses to chronic pain rather than predisposing personality characteristics that somehow contribute to pain behavior.

Other patient characteristics presumed to be individual in nature may actually reflect the interpersonal setting of pain behavior. It is difficult, for example, for patients to be "dependent" unless their family or medical system provides support (Gentry et al., 1974; Roy, Bellissimo, & Tunks, 1982). Similarly, patients cannot adopt a "sick role" (Gallagher & Wrobel, 1982), which exempts them from their usual obligations and responsibilities, without help from significant others. Thus, the environmental or interpersonal nature of pain behavior is an implicitly accepted component of most conceptualizations and treatment programs.

LINKAGES BETWEEN FAMILY DYNAMICS AND CHRONIC PAIN

Theoretical Considerations

According to Szasz (1955), pain has communicative meanings whenever a second person enters the pain situation. Sometimes a health care provider, but more frequently a family member or significant other, the second person interprets the meaning of the pain (e.g., a request for help, a complaint about unfair treatment, an attack or an attempted retribution) and responds accordingly.

As in most areas involving family systems and health, reciprocal influences are presumed to govern the relationship between families and chronic pain.

Thus, the family may (1) initiate or precipitate chronic pain symptomatology, (2) maintain the symptomatology, or (3) respond to the behavior of a family member with chronic pain. Most research and theoretical work on chronic pain reflects the sophisticated view that the family plays all three of these roles simultaneously and that the maintenance of the pattern is of greater concern than is the etiology of the symptoms.

Fordyce (1976) indicated that people around a pain patient respond to pain behaviors in ways that are positively or negatively reinforcing. Unconscious bargaining or "collusion" (Delvey & Hopkins, 1982) to maintain the patient–care-giver relationship may serve to maintain the chronic pain behavior. This operant conditioning model of the family influence on pain behaviors has been expanded by Mohamed (1982), who observed that family or cultural beliefs and histories affect the selection and maintenance of symptoms. Waring (1977) noted that family members project their mutual desires for connectedness to one another, resulting in dyadic or systemic interactions that facilitate the maintenance of sick role behaviors. As families incorporate such interactions, systems external to the family also respond in ways that reinforce the roles within the family.

When family members become preoccupied with illness behaviors, they may ignore other family relationships. For example, a couple may de-emphasize the marital relationship, particularly when there is marital conflict (Minuchin et al., 1975; Waring, 1977). The decreased marital focus may then serve as an unacknowledged support for the maintenance of individual symptomatology. Children may also maintain their illness behavior in order to hide parental marital conflict (Liebman, Honig, & Berger, 1976).

Roy (1985) identified several marital difficulties that arise when a spouse has chronic pain. For example, the spouses may change roles in ways that not only reinforce the illness behavior, but also lead to shifts in power and self-concept. Communicative behaviors often become indirect, reflecting the frustration, despair, and hostile feelings of both partners. Decreased communicative intimacy coexists with decreased sexual intimacy and increased emotional distress. As this cycle continues, the frustration and guilt of both partners further widen the emotional distance between them.

In these examples, the maintenance of symptoms may protect the stability of the family. The pain complaints, however, are not the result of family dynamics.

Research Relating to Chronic Pain and Families

Research on family involvement with chronic pain has included studies of familial models for pain behavior, the impact of chronic pain on the spouse and/or family, and the relationship between family support and chronic pain.

Familial Models for Chronic Pain. Studies have reported that patients with chronic physical pain are often not the only members of their family with chronic pain. In a study of patients with chronic lower back pain, for example, 59% of the sample of 56 patients reported that at least one other family member had chronic debilitating back pain or another equally debilitating illness (Gentry et al., 1974). Crook and associates (1984) reported that 60% of the persons in their study who claimed to have persistent pain had a parent who also complained of persistent pain. The proportions found in these two studies, however, were not compared to those in families of persons without chronic pain.

In a comparison of patients with painless chronic disease and those with chronic pain, Merskey (1965) found that more pain patients reported family members, including spouses, with chronic pain. In a small sample, Mohamed, Weisz, and Waring (1978) found that depressed pateints with pain reported significantly more family members, including spouses, with pain than did depressed patients with no pain. Similar results were reported by Violon and Giurgea (1984); they found that 78% of chronic pain patients had a family history of chronic pain, compared to 44% of patients with chronic illness without pain. Violon and Giurgea suggested that exposure to pain symptomatology may encourage people to adopt somatic responses to life stresses or to aggravate a potentially minor pain. As an alternative explanation, they postulated that pain perception may be a family-related characteristic.

The Impact of Pain on Family Members. Research on the impact of pain on family members has been limited to studies of marital relationships. Most of the studies have focused on associations between the presence of chronic pain and other characteristics, such as marital satisfaction, sexual dysfunction, and spousal emotional distress. All of the studies have been cross-sectional, involving couples in which chronic pain has already been identified. Thus, the studies document only associations among variables and do not show causality. For example, an association between marital dissatisfaction and chronic pain in one of the spouses does not indicate whether the dissatisfaction occurred prior to the pain onset, arose concomitantly with the increasing pain, or is solely a result of the pain behavior and its sequelae.

Spouses of chronic pain patients have been described with higher than anticipated levels of psychological distress. When Shanfield, Heiman, Cope, and Jones (1979) studied 44 couples in which one member was being treated for chronic pain, they found that spouses of patients had significantly higher scores on the Global Severity Index, a measure of psychological distress, than did nonpatients. As anticipated, patients also had higher scores on this index than did nonpatients. Furthermore, there was a significant relationship between the scores of patients and spouses, suggesting that (1) individuals with similar backgrounds, including level of psychological distress, may choose one another for marriage; or (2) high psychological distress levels in both partners may arise from marital dissatisfaction or reactions to the presence of pain.

In an attempt to determine the impact of chronic pain on spouses, Rowat and Knafl (1985) interviewed 40 spouses of patients who were undergoing treatment for chronic pain. Asked about the amount of distress that they experienced as a direct result of the patients' pain, 12 spouses reported high distress, and 13 spouses reported low distress. High-distressed spouses were more likely to perceive the level of pain as the patients perceived it than were low-distressed spouses; in fact, 50% of the spouses in the high-distressed group rated the pain higher than the patient did. Although the patients' assessment of pain was not different in the two groups, the spouses in the low-distressed group described the pain as less severe than did spouses in the high-distressed group. Thus, perception of spousal pain seems to be related to the degree of perceived psychological stress and effects on family life. In addition, 60% of all spouses were uncertain about the etiology or persistence of the pain, yet the low-distressed spouses felt more knowledgeable than did the high-distressed spouses about the factors that exacerbated or relieved the pain. Thus, spouses and families with a sense of some personal control over pain and pain stressors may be less negatively affected by chronic pain than are families without a sense of personal control.

Kerns and Turk (1984) studied the interrelationships between pain, depression, and marital satisfaction in 30 male chronic pain patients and their wives. Results documented the frequency of depression and marital dissatisfaction in the patients, as well as the frequency of marital dissatisfaction in their wives. In more than 50% of the sample, both spouses reported marital dissatisfaction, with one-third of the couples reporting severe levels of dissatisfaction. Kerns and Turk hypothesized that the pain problem may disrupt marital support and, thus, contribute to the development and maintenance of depression.

Maruta, Osborne, Swanson, and Halling (1981), in a study of 50 pain patients and their spouses, noted the couples' agreement that their marriages had been satisfactory before the onset of pain. After the onset of pain, however, spousal differences emerged. A high proportion of spouses rated the marriage below average, while the majority of patients rated the marriage average or above average. This research also addressed the relationship between chronic pain and sexual activity. Reduction of sexual activity was reported by 62% of patients and by 68% of spouses, while elimination of sexual activity was reported by 16% of both groups. With retrospective questions, 80% of both patients and spouses reported sexual satisfaction prior to the onset of pain. After the onset of pain, only one-third of the couples reported satisfaction with sexual adjustment; one-half expressed dissatisfaction.

In an earlier study, Maruta and Osborne (1978) studied the sexual satisfaction of 66 patients in an inpatient pain management center. More than 50% of the patients reported deterioration in both frequency and quality of sexual activity following the onset of pain. In addition, 50% of the patients reported sexual dysfunction after the onset of the pain problem.

As these studies show, spouses of pain patients generally report depression and other measures of psychological distress, marital dissatisfaction, and sexual dysfunction. Such negative effects of chronic pain on the family may be greater when the patient has high levels of pain and when the spouse and patient feel that they have little control over the pain. In retrospective analyses, both pain patients and their spouses claimed that marital and sexual dissatisfaction increased as a result of the pain. Thus, the pain may be a symptom that becomes reified in the family and blamed for the marital dissatisfaction.

Family Support and Chronic Pain. Many pain control researchers assume that patients who are married and have social support do better in pain control programs than do unmarried and unsupported persons (Sternbach, 1974). This relationship becomes more complex when the quality of the spousal relationship is examined, however.

In an experimental procedure, Block (1981) found that spouses respond physiologically to patient expressions of pain. When spouses of hospitalized pain patients viewed videotapes of the patient's pained and neutral facial expressions, the spouses exhibited greater increases in skin conductance measures for pained than for neutral expressions. Spouses who were more satisfied with their marriage had greater skin conductance increases than did spouses who were less satisfied. The physiological differences did not seem to be related to perception of spousal pain, because satisfied and dissatisfied spouses rated the perceived pain similarly. Block suggested that more highly satisfied spouses may be more empathic and, therefore, inadvertently more solicitous of pain behavior in the patients; thus, they may be reinforcing a pain behavior cycle.

Block, Kremer, and Gaylor (1980) asked 20 pain patients to rate their spouses according to the amount of attention that the spouses paid to pain behavior. Then, they interviewed the patients under two conditions: (1) when observed by their spouses and (2) when observed by a ward clerk (i.e., a neutral observer). Patients with solicitous spouses reported higher levels of pain when their spouses observed them than when the ward clerk observed them, while patients with nonsolicitous spouses reported lower levels of pain when their spouses observed them than when the ward clerk observed them. Patients with solicitous spouses also had a significantly longer duration of pain complaints than did patients with less solicitous spouses. The authors suggested two possible interpretations of these results. First, patients may be more likely to develop chronic pain problems when spouses reinforce the symptoms.

Second, as the pain problem continues, many spouses may adapt to the situation and respond reinforcingly, or they may leave the marriage.

Block and Boyer (1984) further investigated the relationship between chronic pain and spouse response with 51 spouses of hospitalized pain patients. These spouses completed questionnaires about their perception of the spouse's disease (The Spouse's Perception of Disease (SPOD)), a measure of emotional and psychological functioning (Symptom Check List (SCL-90)), and the Locke-Wallace Marital Adjustment Scale. Higher marital satisfaction for spouses was associated not only with higher psychological functioning, but also with the perception that the patients had severe functional difficulties. The authors suggested that marital satisfaction may facilitate the spouse's adjustment, but may be associated with a marital relationship that reinforces pain behavior.

Swanson and Maruta (1980) asked 100 hospitalized pain patients and their closest relatives to complete questionnaires that focused on the qualities of the patients' pain. Families with the highest patient-relative congruence on perception of pain, as demonstrated on these questionnaires, had the poorest treatment outcome, as demonstrated by clinical evidence. Mutual awareness of the pain problem was not related to the severity of the pain. The authors hypothesized that extreme mutuality in the perception of pain may encourage patients and families to reinforce pain behaviors. This finding appears to be consistent with the theory of Minuchin and associates (1975) that enmeshed families may exhibit somatic behaviors and be difficult to treat.

Because these studies indicate that awareness of spousal pain, higher marital satisfaction, and solicitous behavior may be related to increased pain and poorer treatment outcomes, the clinical notion that effective communication and high marital agreement promote health may be simplistic, if not erroneous. Therapists should realize, however, that *reported* marital satisfaction may not reflect the unacknowledged resentment and anger that pain patients and spouses may covertly exhibit to one another.

Research Findings. Viewed separately, each of the three areas of research seems to reflect a single-focus model of the relationship between family dynamics and chronic pain. In the first model, research concerning family histories focuses on predisposing family factors that may encourage a family to reinforcingly attend to a member's pain behavior. In the second model, data on the impact of chronic pain on spouses represent data on the impact of chronic pain on all family members. In the third model, the family's role as a reinforcing or maintaining agent is the focus of studies.

Most of the cited researchers advocate systemic conceptualizations of the relationship between chronic pain and families. Research about families and chronic pain is still in its early stages, however, and methodological difficulties encourage the study of linear, rather than reciprocal, interactions. None of the studies conducted so far support causality in any direction or demonstrate etiology. Yet when considered together, they are consistent with systemic, mutually reinforcing model of pain and family function. This model is the basis for treatment strategies.

IMPLICATIONS FOR TREATMENT

Most pain treatment programs that involve families incorporate aspects of the operant conditioning or behavioral models described by Fordyce (1976) and Sternbach (1974). In behavioral models, an important distinction is made between the concept that pain behavior is reinforced and, to some extent, learned and the belief that pain is unreal, or exists only in the patient's head. Treatment goals are to help patients increase their satisfaction with life in spite of the pain, develop more effective ways of coping with the pain, decrease their dependence on medication and use of health care services, and regain the capabilities and activities that they have discarded as a result of the pain. Patients are active participants in the process and are informed about the goals of treatment and the rationale for success.

In the program described by Fordyce (1976), patients are taught how social learning and experience can influence physiological processes, for example, how certain words can cause salivation. Patients are then taught that learning can also be used to reduce and eliminate physiological responses, such as pain. It is not necessary to manipulate or trick patients into negative reinforcement of pain. In fact, claiming that patients should know that they are teaching themselves to respond to different reinforcers and that pain behavior can be unlearned, Fordyce stressed the role of candor. Fordyce also noted that the program will not be effective unless a spouse or significant other participates with the patient.

A number of techniques can be utilized to help patients decrease pain experiences and learn to live with pain. For example, exercise may be decreased to the level that is not followed by pain and then gradually increased to break an exercise-pain cycle. Another method, the "pain cocktail," may be used to reduce the use of medication. All medications are taken in a sweet syrup. Because the ingestion of the syrup brings pain relief, the syrup itself becomes associated with relief. Gradually, the amount of medication in the cocktail is decreased and frequently may be eliminated completely. Spouses or significant others are also taught to attend to healthy, active behaviors and to ignore pain behaviors.

Outcome Studies

The number of outcome studies on behavioral family treatment of chronic pain patients is limited. Khatami and Rush (1978) described the treatment and follow-up of five patients who were treated with a combination of behavioral and cognitive methods. Behaviorally oriented therapy was used to teach the patients symptom control, primarily through biofeedback or stress reduction techniques. Cognitively oriented therapy was used to help patients change the way that they evaluated and responded to pain and other stressful events. Family members also were taught to modify their reinforcing behaviors. After an average of 35 weekly 1-hour therapy sessions, these patients had significant decreases in pain, hopelessness, depression, and medication use. The benefits had been maintained at 6- and 12-month follow-up evaluations.

Hudgens (1979) described the treatment of 24 pain patients who were hospitalized for 7 to 9 weeks as part of their treatment program. Family members initially worked with a social worker at the hospital for two or three weekly 1-hour sessions and then participated in couple and family sessions. Family members were taught to reinforce healthy behaviors instead of pain-related behaviors. Goals were to increase family interactions around issues other than pain, improve family relationships, regain occupational roles, eliminate the use of pain medication, increase exercise, and reduce the use of health care services. At discharge, two-thirds of the patients reported greater satisfaction with family life, and three-quarters reported a significant increase in recreation and leisure time in the family. No patients were taking pain medication at discharge, and 83% returned to some useful form of work, paid or unpaid, after treatment. Each patient demonstrated age-appropriate activity levels, and 83% of patients and families used the health care system appropriately, according to their physician's report. At follow-up 6 to 24 months later, 18 patients (75%) had maintained their goals. Of the six patients who did not maintain their goals, three were widows living alone, and two had spouses who did not change their patterns of reinforcement.

Roberts and Reinhardt (1980) compared 26 pain patients treated in an 8-week inpatient treatment program with 20 patients who were rejected for treatment in the program and 12 patients who refused to participate in the program. Patients were not admitted to the program if they did not have a significant other willing to work with them or if they had associated medical, mental, or alcohol problems. In the program, patients learned behavioral techniques to cope with their pain, and family members learned to modify their rewarding responses. Successful outcome at a 1-month follow-up consisted of appropriate employment, no disability compensation, and no medication. Although there were no differences between the treated and nontreated groups in the assessment of pain at entry, successful outcome was reported by

77% of the treated group, by only one patient in the group rejected for treatment, and by none of those who refused treatment.

According to Waring (1980, 1982), a cognitive model enables family members to understand the reciprocal influences that maintain symptoms such as chronic pain, because such a model specifically suppresses affect. Waring noted that the work of Minuchin and associates (1975) suggests that the families most likely to exhibit psychosomatic symptoms may be very uncomfortable with therapeutic styles that encourage displays of affect and emotional catharsis. Using clinical anecdotes, Waring (1982) described how marital intimacy is increased with cognitive self-disclosure and how this increase in intimacy is accompanied by decreases in pain complaints.

Liebman, Honig, and Berger (1976), in a report of therapy for the families of ten children who had been hospitalized for chronic pain, described another therapeutic style that emphasizes family communication. The treatment model focused on decreasing the pain behavior of the children by decreasing their dependence on their child's physician, requiring school attendance, and diminishing the special member role that they held in their family. The attention in the weekly therapy sessions quickly moved to an investigation of family patterns that were maintaining the child's role. In seven of the ten families, significant marital problems surfaced, and the parents were able to shift their attention to the marital relationship. This program was claimed to be effective, as none of the ten children required hospitalization again in a 2-year period.

Outcome studies of family treatment of chronic pain have many methodological problems: the small sample size; the lack of independent evaluations; the lack of comparison groups, particularly those who received other forms of treatment; and the lack of reliable measures. Yet, the behavioral outcomes of the treated groups, especially in the study by Hudgens (1979), are impressive. Given the reciprocal patterns maintained by families, it seems reasonable to assume that the incorporation of family members into a treatment program, particularly one that emphasizes changes in reinforcement cues, is very worthwhile.

Therapeutic Strategies

Family therapists are likely to incorporate multiple therapeutic strategies into their treatment of families that have a member with chronic pain. Families that have participated in chronic pain treatment programs probably understand behavioral techniques, but the therapist may want (1) to help these families consider their responses to the behavioral approaches and (2) to determine whether these responses are enhancing or hindering treatment. In addition, because of a systemic orientation about the ways in which family members cooperate, the therapist is likely to consider the function that the pain serves for the family (i.e., the ways in which pain masks other conflicts or provides justification for patterns of interaction).

When a family first enters treatment, the therapist should discuss the history of the pain and its treatment. In many cases, patients feel that health care professionals and family members have dismissed their pain complaints. The frustration and accompanying anger are often shared by all family members. It may be very important for the therapist to acknowledge these feelings (Engel, 1959; Jeans & Rowat, 1984). In working with the family to decrease pain behaviors and increase family satisfaction, therapists must also consider their own responses so that they do not inadvertently participate in familiar patterns such as "blaming the victim" or deifying the martyred family member.

In addition to their resentment toward the health care system, family members frequently feel resentment toward one another. The identified patient may feel that he or she receives too little support or else too much attention and is, therefore, hesitant to raise other concerns. In most families, the care-giving persons benefit from their responsible role, but they may also have concerns about their capabilities and limitations in the care-giving role.

Families may cope with these reciprocal concerns by discussing them continuously, thus paying less attention to or even avoiding other family and individual problems. In such cases, treatment may focus less on the emotional responses and more on the development of other interaction patterns. Alternatively, and perhaps more frequently, family members may not discuss their fears and frustrations with one another, and the family therapist may encourage affective and emotional responses. Because the feelings of anger, resentment, fear of intimacy, and fear of death that may be expressed can be very frightening for both the family and the therapist, a careful therapeutic balancing act may be necessary to enable families to discuss their fears and responses to pain openly, but simultaneously to discourage the "triangulation" of the pain in the family members' interactions.

Family concerns may be exacerbated because of the feelings of hopelessness that result from the frustrating and chronic nature of physical pain (Jeans & Rowat, 1984). One such concern is trust, particularly the question of whether the patient and family members believe one another about the characteristics of the pain. The therapist and family should explore the familial and cultural meanings of pain, perhaps with the use of a genogram, in order to obtain specific information about the family's beliefs.

Therapy may address the family's expectations about intimacy. The family may need to examine the differences between the needs of the identified patient and the needs of the other family members and the family as a unit. It is important to initiate discussions of sexuality in couples in which a member has chronic pain. Maruta and Osborne (1978) noted that physicians who routinely asked their chronic pain patients about sexual problems encountered nearly twice as many patients who admitted such problems as did physicians who did not ask. This indicated that sexual satisfaction may be an area of concern, but not an area that families feel free to discuss.

Family therapy for chronic pain is not generally undertaken without concomitant medical treatment. Unfortunately, medical treatment is undertaken without accompanying family therapy more frequently. Based on the information reviewed in this paper, it is suggested that medical treatment also not be undertaken without consideration of the family context of the pain patient. The proliferation and success of pain clinics reflects a model in which both medical treatment and family-oriented therapy can be integrated.

Sometimes, families seek therapy themselves or are referred to a therapist by a physician as a "last resort." In such situations, the therapist should consider himself or herself a part of the treatment team and should maintain a systemic orientation about the nature of the "treatment family." There should be some form of contact between the therapist and the physician so that assessment, treatment, and follow-up can be coordinated and consistent. Hepworth and Jackson (1985) have identified several forms of therapist-physician collaboration that might be implemented.

The relationship between family dynamics and chronic pain is obviously complex and dependent on many social, individual, and familial factors. It serves as a useful model for the relationship between family dynamics and health, however, because it is a common condition of concern to both families and health care providers in which the role of the family is recognized. Rather than on the assignment of individual blame or the identification of etiology, treatment focuses on the patterns of family interaction that co-exist with chronic pain and serve to maintain symptoms. Thus, family therapists are likely to continue to attend to this condition in order to increase their understanding of the reciprocal and ongoing influences of family dynamics and specific areas of health.

REFERENCES

Bergman, J., & Werblun, M. (1978). Chronic pain: A review for the family physician. *The Journal of Family Practice, 7,* 685–693.

Block, A. (1981). An investigation of the response of the spouse to chronic pain behavior. *Psychosomatic Medicine, 43,* 415–422.

Block, A., & Boyer, S. (1984). The spouse's adjustment to chronic pain: Cognitive and emotional factors. *Social Science and Medicine, 19,* 1313–1317.

Block, A., Kremer, E., & Gaylor, M. (1980). Behavioral treatment of chronic pain: The spouse as a discriminative cue for pain behavior. *Pain, 9,* 243–252.

Crook, J., Rideout, E., & Browne, G. (1984). The prevalence of pain complaints in a general population. *Pain, 18,* 299–314.

Delvey, J., & Hopkins, L. (1982). Pain patients and their partners: The role of collusion in chronic pain. *Journal of Marital and Family Therapy, 8,* 135–142.

Engel, G. (1959). Psychogenic pain and the pain prone patient. *American Journal of Medicine, 26,* 899.

Fordyce, W. (1976). *Behavioral methods for chronic pain and illness.* St. Louis: C.V. Mosby.

Gallagher, E. & Wrobel, S. (1982). The sick-role and chronic pain. In R. Roy & E. Tunks (Eds.), *Chronic pain: Psychosocial factors in rehabilitation.* Baltimore: Williams & Wilkins.

Gentry, W.D., Shows, W.D., & Thomas, M. (1974). Chronic low back pain: A psychological profile. *Psychosomatics, 15,* 174–177.

Greenhoot, J., & Sternbach, R. (1977). Conjoint treatment of chronic pain. In A. Jacox (Ed.), *A source book for nurses and other health professionals* (pp 295–302). Boston: Little, Brown.

Hepworth, J. (1987). A boy with abdominal pain. In W.J. Doherty & M. Baird (Eds.), *Case studies in family-centered medical care.* New York: Guilford Press.

Hepworth, J., & Jackson, M. (1985). Health care for families: Models of collaboration between family therapists and family physicians. *Family Relations, 34,* 123–127.

Hudgens, A. (1979). Family-oriented treatment of chronic pain. *Journal of Marital and Family Therapy, 5,* 67–78.

Jeans, M., & Rowat, K. (1984). Counselling the patient and family. In R. Wall and R. Melzack (Eds.), *Textbook of pain* (pp. 795–798). London: Churchill Livingstone.

Kerns, R., & Turk, D. (1984). Depression and chronic pain: The mediating role of the spouse. *Journal of Marriage and the Family, 46,* 845–852.

Khatami, M., & Rush, J. (1978). A pilot study of the treatment of outpatients with chronic pain: Symptom control, stimulus control and social system intervention. *Pain, 5,* 163–172.

Liebman, R., Honig, P., & Berger, H. (1976). An integrated treatment program for psychogenic pain. *Family Process, 15,* 397–405.

Maruta, T., & Osborne, D. (1978). Sexual activity in chronic pain patients. *Psychosomatics, 19,* 531–537.

Maruta, T., Osborne, D., Swanson, D., & Halling, J. (1981). Chronic pain patients and spouses. *Mayo Clinic Proceedings, 56,* 307–310.

Merskey, J. (1965). Psychiatric patients with persistent pain. *Journal of Psychosomatic Research, 9,* 299–309.

Minuchin, S., Baker, L., Rosman, B.L., Liebman, R., Milman, L., & Todd, T. (1975) A conceptual model for psychosomatic illness in children: Family organization and family therapy. *Archives of General Psychiatry, 32,* 1031–1038.

Mohamed, S. (1982). The patient and his family. In R. Roy & E. Tunks (Eds.), *Chronic pain: Psychosocial factors in rehabilitation.* Baltimore: Williams & Wilkins.

Mohamed, S., Weisz, G., & Waring, E. (1978). The relationship of chronic pain to depression, marital adjustment, and family dynamics. *Pain, 5,* 285–292.

Roberts, A., & Reinhardt, L. (1980). The behavioral management of chronic pain: Long-term follow-up with comparison groups. *Pain, 8,* 151–162.

Rowat, K., & Knafl, K. (1985). Living with chronic pain: The spouse's perspective. *Pain, 23,* 259–271.

Roy, R. (1984). Chronic pain: A family perspective. *International Journal of Family Therapy, 6,* 31–43.

Roy, R. (1985). Chronic pain and marital difficulties. *Health & Social Work, 10,* 199–207.

Roy, R., Bellissimo, A., Tunks, E. (1982). The chronic pain patient and the environment. In R. Roy & E. Tunks (Eds.), *Chronic pain: Psychosocial factors in rehabilitation*. Baltimore: Williams & Wilkins.

Shanfield, S., & Killingsworth, R. (1977). The psychiatric aspects of pain. *Psychiatric Annals, 7,* 24–35.

Shanfield, S., Heiman, E., Cope, D., & Jones, J. (1979). Pain and the marital relationship: Psychiatric distress. *Pain, 7,* 343–351.

Sternbach, R. (1974). *Pain patients: Traits & treatment*. New York. Academic Press.

Swanson, D., & Maruta, R. (1980). The family's viewpoint of chronic pain. *Pain, 8,* 163–166.

Szasz, T. (1955). The nature of pain. *Archives of Neurology & Psychiatry, 74,* 174–181.

Violon, A., & Giurgea, D. (1984). Familial models for chronic pain. *Pain, 18,* 199–203.

Waring, E. (1980). Family therapy and psychosomatic illness. *International Journal of Family Therapy, 2,* 243–252.

Waring, E. (1977). The role of the family in symptom selection and perpetuation in psychosomatic illness. *Psychotherapy and Psychosomatics, 28,* 253–259.

Waring, E. (1982). Conjoint marital and family therapy. In R. Roy & E. Tunks (Eds.), *Chronic pain: Psychosocial factors in rehabilitation* (pp. 151–165). Baltimore: Williams & Wilkins.

Weakland, J. (1977). Family somatics: A neglected edge. *Family Process, 16,* 263–272.

5. Therapy with Families of Children with Sickle Cell Disease

Barbara S. Nevergold, PhD
Director
Foster Care Adoption Program
Friendship House of Western New York, Inc.
Buffalo, New York

Sickle cell anemia is a disease with "family connections" that span countless generations. Ancient folklore contains numerous references to conditions likely to be sickle cell anemia. Furthermore, many African tribes have demonstrated a clear understanding of the symptoms associated with sickle cell anemia and have specific names for this ailment in their vocabularies. In fact, sickle cell disease has been identified as the most common genetic disorder known to man (Rooks & Pack, 1983).

The incidence of sickle cell trait and sickle cell anemia among African-Americans has been well documented. The trait is found to occur in approximately 10% of African-Americans, whereas sickle cell anemia strikes 1 in 400 to 500 individuals (Francis, Wethers, & Fenwick, 1970; Scott & Uy, 1977). A combined incidence rate for all forms of sickle cell disease has been calculated to be 4.6/1,000 live African-American births (Gortmacher & Sappenfield, 1984). In the United States, there are presently more than 50,000 African-Americans afflicted with sickle cell anemia; several thousand more have either sickle hemoglobin C disease or sickle beta-thalassemia. Sickle cell disease has also been found to occur among Italians, Greeks, Arabs, and Asians. In spite of the long history of sickle cell disease, only recently has it been recognized that this chronic illness severely stresses the family, as well as the individual sufferer.

In a recent report, Hobbs, Perrin, Ireys, Moynihan, and Shayne (1983) briefly outlined the impact that the severe chronic illnesses of childhood, including sickle cell disease, have on the family and its members. They characterized these families as:

burdened with caring responsibilities, affected by anxiety and sometimes guilt, strapped by unpredictable expenses and possibly economic ruin, and facing an uncertain future that often includes the
premature death of the child. (p. 2)

While the authors emphasized that their major concern was with public
policies that affect chronically ill children and their families, they identified a
number of the stressors that threaten the integrity of the family with a
chronically ill child. There are internal stressors that result from interpersonal
relations of family members (e.g., marital strain, difficulties in parent-child
relations, and sibling conflict) and external or environmental stressors that
result from the family's relations with outside agencies, such as hospitals,
schools, or social service agencies. In spite of the diversity of the illnesses cited,
the authors emphasized the commonality of the stresses that families with
chronically ill children experience.

Steinhauer, Mushin, and Rae-Grant (1974) found that the chronic illness
of a child is likely to intensify stress on the family. Furthermore, the intensity of
the stress is related to the severity of the illness, the nature of the illness (i.e.,
congenital or acquired), and the extent to which emotional disturbances
preexist in the family. Sickle cell disease is a lifelong, life-threatening, and
often unpredictable disease that may continually challenge the family's adaptive capability.

Family therapy is often indicated for the families of children with sickle cell
disease. In order to ensure a comprehensive approach to the provision of
health care services to these children and their families, it is wise to include a
family therapist as a member of the management team. While family therapists
are accustomed to working with families that find it difficult to cope with the
stresses associated with normal developmental stages, therapists must overcome additional barriers in working with a family that has a child with sickle
cell disease. For example, therapists must

- have a knowledge of the nature of sickle cell disease, including an understanding of the genetic significance and the physical complications of the
  disease
- understand the impact of the disease on the child's emotional and social
  adjustment
- distinguish between the stresses that result from the child's illness and
  those that may result from other circumstances
- establish a good collaborative relationship with the family's physician or
  other health care providers responsible for the child's medical care

THE NATURE OF SICKLE CELL DISEASE

The generic term *sickle cell disease* is used to describe all disorders of the red blood cells containing the abnormal hemoglobin designated as hemoglobin S. Sickle cell anemia, the most common and most debilitating form of the disease, is characterized by the presence of two genes for sickle hemoglobin. The other forms of the disease result from the combination of a single gene for sickle hemoglobin and another hemoglobin abnormality, such as hemoglobin C; Beta-thalassemia; hereditary persistence of fetal hemoglobin; and hemoglobin D Punjab, E, G, J, H, and O Arab (Scott & Uy, 1977).

Medical interest in sickle cell disease has a remarkably short history. The first mention of sickled blood cells is found in the writings of Dr. J.B. Herrick in 1910. In 1926, sickle cell disease was differentiated from its carrier state, sickle cell trait, which is an asymptomatic condition. Dr. Linus Pauling is credited with the breakthrough in 1954 that made it possible to differentiate the various hemoglobins and led to the identification of sickle cell disease as a defect in the hemoglobin. While research continues in search of a cure, sickle cell disease is presently incurable.

The symptoms of sickle cell disease appear in the first few months of life. Pallor, anemia, and organomegaly (particularly involving the heart, liver, and spleen) are early signs of the disease (Scott & Uy, 1977). Individuals with sickle cell disease experience unpredictable episodes of severe, sometimes disabling, pain in the joints, abdomen, spine, and other parts of the body. The pain, which may occur monthly or infrequently, may require hospitalization. Pneumonia, bone infections, and jaundice may occur. A major problem is an increased susceptibility to certain infections (Mathur, 1983). The disease may retard growth and sexual development. There is also evidence that it affects fertility. (Jimenez, Scott, Henry, Sampson, & Ferguson, 1966).

The treatment of sickle cell disease is symptomatic. Medication is prescribed to relieve sickle cell crises (i.e., pain episodes), and transfusions are given for symptomatic anemia or severe infections during crises. The course of the disease is variable, however. Not all patients experience the symptoms with the same frequency or severity. The life span of a sickle cell patient is also variable, with many individuals living into their 40s, 50s, or 60s.

The only way that a child can contract sickle cell disease is to inherit it. If both parents have sickle cell trait, there is a 25% chance that their child will inherit the disease. This risk is constant for each pregnancy of this couple. If only one parent has sickle cell trait, however, there is no chance that the child will inherit the disease. The risk of sickle cell disease is 25% higher for a child if one parent has the disease and the other parent has the trait.

LITERATURE REVIEW

The body of literature on sickle cell disease as a source of stress on the family is relatively small. In one of the first articles on the subject, Whitten and Fischhoff (1974) cited several areas in which the family's attempts to cope with sickle cell disease cause stress:

- financial strain
- restrictions on the social life of the parents and the family in general
- neglect of the other children in the family
- parental guilt (over having caused the child's illness)
- transportation problems (to hospital and medical appointments)
- disruptions in family routines
- interruptions of the parents' work schedules

Whitten, Waugh, and Moore (1974) interviewed the mothers of sickle cell anemia patients under the age of 18 years. The interviews were designed to assess the mothers' knowledge, attitudes, feelings, behavior, and experiences related to their child's illness. Almost 25% of the mothers had incomplete or incorrect knowledge about the genetics of the disease. More than one-half of the mothers were unaware of the factors responsible for the anemia in sickle cell anemia. Furthermore, 35% of the mothers did not know why children with sickle cell anemia experience pain. Almost 50% could not adequately describe the difference between sickle cell trait and sickle cell anemia. Half of the mothers could not describe their child's feelings about the disease, which suggests that they had little or no discussion about the illness with the child. Many mothers worried about their child's life expectancy, but had not discussed their fears with their doctors.

In order to study selected psychosocial problems in families of sickle cell anemia patients, Nishiura and Whitten (1980) collected data through structured interviews with 141 parents, who had a total of 162 children with sickle cell anemia. The children ranged from 3 months to 17 years in age. Fifty-one percent of the children were males. Of these families, 27% had incomes of less than $3,000; 12% had incomes of $17,000 or more. Fifty-one percent of the families were headed by a single parent. The principal means of support for 47% of the families was public assistance, Social Security, or sources other than employment.

Nishiura and Whitten (1980) examined six variables: (1) family finances, (2) problems in obtaining medical care, (3) interpersonal relationships within the family, (4) disease adjustment, (5) sexual development, and (6) school achievement. In all families, with the exception of those who had full Medicaid coverage, the medical costs of the child's illness caused some financial strain. Problems in obtaining medical care for the child were related to cost, transportation, parent's time away from work, or the need to find a babysitter for the child's siblings.

Although Nishiura and Whitten (1980) expected to find evidence of stress in marital relationships, the data revealed "relatively few problems in interpersonal relations within families" (p. 34). The authors suggested that this finding may be explained by the fact that only married respondents, 49% of the sample, were questioned about their relationship with their spouses. The authors added that parents may have been reluctant to blame their child's illness for problems among family members. The study did reveal, however, sibling jealousy between the child with sickle cell anemia and other children in the family.

The data in the area of disease adjustment suggested that many children, 25% of the sample, attempted to use their disease to manipulate others. Girls were more likely to do this than were boys. Nishiura and Whitten (1980) found that one-half of the parents worried about the amount of activity that they should allow their child. The parents of nearly 45% of the adolescents (i.e., 12 years and older) believed that their child's physical development was delayed. There appeared to be a lack of communication between parent and child on this subject, however, as 40% of the children in this age group had not discussed sex with their parents.

In regard to school achievement, approximately one-third of the children studied were below their proper grade level. By the time they were in their older teen years, 60% of the sample had repeated one or more grades. This poor school achievement record was attributed to the intermittent absences caused by the unpredictable nature of sickle cell disease. Over one-half of the children reported only fair or poor grades, yet parents of 60% of these children expressed the expectation that their children would complete college. This finding indicates some discrepancy between the parents' expectations and reality.

Two recent studies have focused on families that have a child with sickle cell disease (Burlew, Evans, & Oler, 1985; Nevergold, 1986). Burlew and her associates (1985) conducted a 3-year study to examine family functioning, parents' perceptions of the child's behavior, and parents' perceptions of the parent-child relationship. The sample for this study consisted of 19 couples who had children between the ages of 2 and 5, with sickle cell anemia. A control group of 19 couples whose children did not have a chronic illness were randomly selected from a group of outpatients at the Cincinnati Health Medical Center. The participants were given the following instruments:

1. Child Behavior Trait Scale
2. Me and My Child

3. Parental Affiliation Scale
4. Family Environment Scale (Moos, 1974)
5. Feetham Family Functioning Scale
6. Impact on Family Scale

Although they have not yet completed their analysis of the data, Burlew and her colleagues have released some preliminary results:

1. Parents of children with sickle cell anemia reported less favorable affiliation between themselves than did control parents.
2. There were no differences between the two groups on perceptions of the child's behavior and perceptions of the parent-child interaction.
3. Among the families of children with sickle cell anemia, parents in two-parent families perceived the child's behavior more favorably and reported more favorable parent-child interaction than did single parents. Among control families, there were no such differences.
4. Among the families of children with sickle cell anemia, positive parental affiliation was not significantly associated with perceptions of the child's behavior or perceptions of parent-child interaction.

The preliminary results of the Family Environment Scale were not significant (Burlew, personal communication, September 1985). Although Burlew and her colleagues found the two family groups perceived their environments in the same way, their study did indicate potential marital strain. Plans are to continue the study by expanding the sample size for another year or two.

In a study to examine perceptions of family environment and parent-child relations, as well as to assess the adolescents' level of self-esteem, Nevergold (1986) focused on adolescents with sickle cell disease and their parents. Twenty adolescents with sickle cell disease and their parents were compared to a group of healthy adolescents and their parents. Both adolescents and parents were given the Family Environment Scale (Moos, 1974) and the Parent-Child Relationship Questionnaire (Roe & Siegelman, 1963). Only the adolescents were given the Tennessee Self Concept Scale (Fitts, 1965).

As in the earlier study (Burlew et al., 1985), Nevergold found no significant differences in the two groups' perceptions of their family environment. Mothers of children with sickle cell disease saw their relationships with their children as more loving than did the comparison mothers, but there were no significant differences on the measure for either the adolescents or their fathers. The findings on the self-concept measure were consistent with previous research in that the adolescents with sickle cell disease were found to have a lower self-esteem than did their peers.

The development of a positive self-image is a complex process. The response of the children to their physical disability, as well as that of other family members, enters into this process. Overprotective parents, for example, deny their child opportunities to master elements of the environment and thereby contribute to the child's feelings of dependency and lowered self-esteem.

PSYCHOLOGICAL EFFECTS OF SICKLE CELL DISEASE

The body of literature on the psychological effects of sickle cell disease on the child and adolescent is more extensive than that on the family.

On the Child

It has been well documented that children with sickle cell disease are more vulnerable to emotional problems than are their healthy peers. As Whitten and Fischhoff (1974) observed, "it is well established that long term physical disorder can lead to a social disability far more serious than the physical problem" (p. 681).

As mentioned earlier, the self-esteem of children and adolescents with sickle cell disease is almost always lower than that of their healthy counterparts (Conyard, Krishnamurthy, & Dosik, 1980; Glanville, 1978; Kumar, Powars, Allen, & Haywood, 1976; LePontois, 1975; Nevergold, 1986; Williams, Earles, & Pack, 1983). Furthermore, younger children often exhibit feelings of helplessness, fear of abandonment, and dependency. Adolescents may withdraw from relationships; have limited aspirations and motivations; be afraid to be autonomous; and feel depressed, helpless, fearful, and preoccupied with death. Adolescents, in particular, are vulnerable to problems of low self-esteem, dependency, and slow social maturation.

Whitten and Nishiura (1985) have identified several sources of the emotional stress experienced by a child with sickle cell disease. They found that stress often resulted from (1) the pain and other physical complications of the disease, (2) anxiety about treatment procedures and fear of unfamiliar medical facilities, and (3) the emotional climate created by the child's family. Family members may be overly indulgent and/or resentful toward the child as a result of the burdens placed on them by the illness. In addition, the threat of physical impairment, shortened life expectancy, and interruptions of the child's normal activities contribute to the stress.

On the Family

In many respects, the families of children with sickle cell disease resemble the families of children affected by other chronic illnesses. For example, the family's life may often center around the affected child, and the family system may be organized to accommodate the demands of the sick child. Parental behavior in child-rearing may take several forms along a continuum from overprotection to rejection, although the most common behavior is to overprotect the child.

In most cases, parents first learn that they are both carriers of the sickle cell gene following the birth of their affected child. They most frequently respond with anger because this happened to them and their child; denial because the baby looks healthy and symptoms do not appear until the sixth month or so; and self-blame and guilt or spousal blame because they caused their child's illness. Some parents adopt a fatalistic acceptance of the child's disease as a matter of God's will. As future pregnancies may be seen in the same light, family planning may not take into consideration the 25% chance that the next child may also inherit the disease.

Often, parents must deal with a complex medical system that may be overwhelming to them. In addition, they must give up the control of their child's life to physicians and other health care providers. The parents may develop a sense of helplessness because of their inability to protect their child from the symptoms of the disease. The helplessness is exacerbated by the unpredictability of pain episodes and other complications, the frequency of hospitalizations, and the incurable nature of sickle cell disease.

Children with sickle cell disease may have a difficult time moving through the developmental tasks necessary to establish their own autonomy and independence from their parents. Since this disease affects growth, development, and sexual maturation, many children are smaller in stature and size than are their peers. Parents may be reluctant to see their child behave in an age-appropriate manner and to allow the child the experiences necessary to develop independence. This is particularly true for adolescents.

There is a lack of knowledge and understanding about the myriad of biopsychosocial complications of this disease, both in the African-American community and the community at large. Parents and patients are often unaware of the ramifications of the disease, but are afraid to ask questions of the doctors or hesitate to admit their own anxieties. Many parents are reluctant to let others in the community know about their child's illness, because they believe that their child will be stigmatized. Therefore, they do not always make use of support systems outside their family.

THERAPEUTIC INTERVENTION

Stress on the family and its members can be considered inevitable. Minuchin (1974) theorized that the family is subject to pressures from both internal and external sources. He identified four sources of stress on the family: (1) contacts of an individual family member with extrafamilial forces, (2) contacts of the family as a whole with extrafamilial forces, (3) the family's passage through developmental points in its life cycle, and (4) problems that are idiosyncratic to the family. The areas of stress experienced by families of children with sickle cell disease fall into the broad categories identified by Minuchin. The categories are not mutually exclusive, and these families may experience stress from one or more sources.

Families that cope successfully with stress develop adaptational styles that are open to change (Minuchin, 1974). Families that have difficulty coping with stress are families that resist or are unable to adapt to change. In order to avoid or resist the alternatives, these families increase the rigidity of their transactional patterns or boundaries and may develop dysfunctional transactional patterns.

Robert M. is a 21-year-old who has sickle cell anemia. His mother and father are divorced, and Robert has not seen his father since he was 6 years old, when Mrs. M. moved to her present home in a different city following the divorce. Robert also lives with his older brother John, aged 23, and his younger sister Antoinette, aged 19, neither of whom have the disease or the trait. Mrs. M. has been screened and has sickle cell trait. Mr. M. was never tested.

At birth, Robert weighed 7 pounds, 3 ounces. He had no medical problems until the age of 8 months, when he had his first painful crisis in his hands and feet. The diagnosis of sickle cell anemia was made at this time. Mrs. M. was incredulous; not only had she not known very much about this disease, but also she could not recall anyone in her family who had this disease. Her husband was not much help, as he refused to be tested or to discuss his family history with the doctors. Later, Mrs. M. recalled that her husband's father and older sister had been sickly all their lives with an ailment vaguely described as "bad blood." No one had ever used the term *sickle cell anemia*, however.

During the first 2 or 3 years for his life, Robert had multiple episodes of painful swelling of his hands and feet. He was hospitalized eight times during this period. For the next 5 years, however, he had fewer painful episodes and required only four hospitalizations. He had a healthy appetite, but did not grow very much during these years. At age 8, his height and weight were in the 3rd percentile for his age group. He had a recurrent problem of enuresis, but the findings of a urological examination were normal.

Between the ages of 9 and 12, Robert had four or five painful crises in his abdomen and extremities. While not requiring hospitalization, each was severe enough to keep him home from school. Between the ages of 12 and 16, Robert continued to have one or two painful crises each year that did not require hospitalization, but he also had an average of three episodes each year in which the pain lasted more than 36 hours and did require hospitalization. His school attendance was erratic. While IQ tests indicated above average intelligence, Robert's school performance was marginal. His teachers described him as withdrawn and difficult to reach. He appeared to have no friends among his classmates. His teachers felt that he was extremely sensitive about his small stature. At the age of 16, he looked more like a 10-year-old.

From age 16 until the time that the family was referred for counseling, Robert had continued to have pain episodes that interfered with school attendance, although the hospitalizations averaged only one a year. He graduated from high school at age 20, two years behind his class and in the bottom quarter academically. He had been looking for work, against the wishes of his mother. Mrs. M. felt that her son was not strong enough to work full-time. Both of the other children agreed with their mother.

At the time the family was referred for counseling, the issue of Robert's working had become the major focal point of family arguments. Robert's response to his family's opposition to his working was to begin to abuse his medication. A prescription for pain medication that had previously lasted 1 month now had to be refilled after 2 weeks. When he began to call his doctor and ask for prescriptions every week, the doctor became alarmed and referred the family to the family therapist.

The therapist employed various interventions within the framework of Minuchin's structural family therapy. During the initial sessions, the therapist used the technique of enactment to help identify the family's transactional patterns. It became apparent that the family's stress was related to the way in which the family had dealt with Robert's sickle cell anemia. Family members were enmeshed, rarely doing things independently, and Robert was the focal point of their activities. His mother and siblings had formed a coalition to protect Robert and to cater to his needs. Citing his illness as the reason, they refused to allow him to do any household chores. They perceived him as fragile and unable to do any work, even if it were not strenuous. They had, therefore, effectively prevented Robert from developing autonomy and were keeping him dependent on the family. Robert's insistence on finding a job was the first serious attempt he had made to disengage from the family.

The therapist worked with the family on two levels. He assigned family members several tasks in which they were instructed to let Robert assume responsibility for several household tasks. They were also instructed to plan one or two activities that did not require the participation of every family member. Consulting Robert's doctor, the therapist ascertained that, while Robert's illness did prohibit his employment in certain jobs, working was not out of the question. The therapist set up an appointment for Robert and his mother to discuss Robert's physical limitations with the doctor, instructing them to prepare a list of questions for the doctor beforehand. Mrs. M. admitted that she always became anxious when discussing Robert's case with his doctor and was afraid to ask blunt questions about Robert's capabilities. She was afraid that she was not prepared to hear some of the doctor's responses to her questions. Following the session with the doctor, the therapist encouraged Robert to share what he had learned with his siblings. John and Antoinette began to see that Robert was able to take responsibility for managing his illness.

The therapist also referred Robert to the Office of Vocational Rehabilitation, where a counselor gave Robert a series of vocational and psychological tests as part of a job readiness assessment. Finding that Robert had good hand-eye coordination and good mathematical skills, the counselor arranged for Robert to be placed in an on-the-job training program with a local bank. Initially, Robert would work evenings in a clerical position as a check sorter. Later, he would be given an opportunity to train as a teller.

The family therapist continued to work with the family throughout the restructuring process. During this time, Robert's doctor reported that his use of pain medication had returned to its normal level. Robert's successful completion of the training program marked the termination of therapy.

CONCLUSION

Families of children who have a chronic illness, such as sickle cell disease, are prone to stress because of the complexities of raising these children. Often, the stress of normal developmental stages is intensified or prolonged. In the case of Robert, neither his mother nor his siblings were able to view him as an adult; they continued to see him as a sick child in need of their protection. While family therapy with the family of a child with sickle cell disease is not necessarily different from therapy with families of healthy children, the family therapist must recognize that a working knowledge of the nature of the illness and its impact on the family is essential to successful therapy.

REFERENCES

Burlew, K., Evans, R., & Oler, C. (1985). The impact of a child with sickle cell anemia on family dynamics and interactions. *Proceedings of 1985 National Conference, Sickle Cell Disease: Progress of the Eighties.* Los Angeles Department of Health, Los Angeles, California.

Conyard, S., Krishnamurthy, M., & Dosik, H. (1980). Psychosocial aspects of sickle cell anemia in adolescents. *Health Social Work, 5,* 20–26.

Fitts, W.H. (1965). *Manual: Tennessee self-concept scale.* Nashville, TN: Counselor Recording and Tests.

Francis, Y., Wethers, D.L., Fenwick, L.A. (1970). The Foundation for Research and Education in Sickle Cell Disease: A prospective. *Journal of the National Medical Association, 62*(3), 200–203.

Glanville, S.M. (1978). *A comparison of emotional and behavioral adjustment among children with sickle cell anemia, diabetes mellitus, and normal physical development.* Unpublished doctoral dissertation. The Louisiana State University of Agricultural & Mechanical College.

Gortmacher, S., & Sappenfield, W. (1984). Chronic childhood disorders: Prevalence and impact. *Pediatric Clinics of North America, 31*(1), 3–17.

Hobbs, N., Perrin, J.M., Ireys, H., Moynihan, L., & Shayne, M.W. (1983). *Chronically ill children in America: Background and recommendations.* Nashville, TN: Vanderbilt Institute for Public Policy Studies.

Jimenez, C., Scott, R., Henry, W.L., Sampson, C., Ferguson, A. (1966). The effects of hemoglobin C sickle cell disease on the onset of menarche, pregnancy, fertility, pubescent changes, and body growth in Negro subjects. *American Journal of Disease in Children, 111,* 497–504.

Kumar, S., Powars, D., Allen, J., & Haywood, J. (1976). Anxiety, self-concept, and personal and social adjustments in children with sickle cell anemia. *Adolescent Medicine, 88*(5), 859–863.

LePontois, J. (1975). Adolescents with sickle cell anemia deal with life and death. *Social Work in Health Care, 1*(1), 71–80.

Mathur, L.R. (1983). Sickle cell anemia: New approaches to therapy. *Research Resources Reporter, 7*(10).

Minuchin, S. (1974). *Families and family therapy.* Cambridge, MA: Harvard University Press.

Moos, R.H. (1974). *The family environment.* Palo Alto, CA: Consulting Psychologist Press, Inc.

Nevergold, B.S. (1986). *Sickle cell disease and its effect on parental relations, family environment and self-perceptions of black adolescents.* Unpublished doctoral dissertation. State University of New York, Buffalo.

Nishiura, E., & Whitten, C. (1980). Psychosocial problems in families of children with sickle cell anemia. *Urban Health,* 32–35.

Roe, A., Siegelman, M. (1963). A parent-child relations questionnaire. *Child Development, 34,* 355–359.

Rooks, Y., & Pack B. (1983). A profile of sickle cell disease. *Nursing Clinics of North America, 18*(1), 131–138.

Scott, R.B., & Uy, C. (1977). Sickle cell anemia. *Medical Times.*

Steinhauer, P.D., Mushin, D., & Rae-Grant, Q. (1974). Psychological aspects of chronic illness. *Pediatric Clinics of North America, 21*(4), 835–840.

Whitten, C., & Fischhoff, J. (1974). Psychosocial effects of sickle cell disease. *Archives of Internal Medicine, 133,* 681–689.

Whitten, C.F., & Nishiura, E.N. (1985). Sickle cell anemia: Public policy issues. In N. Hobbs & J. Perrin (Eds.), *Issues in the care of children with chronic illness.* San Francisco: Jossey-Bass.

Whitten, C., Waugh, D., & Moore, A. (1974). Unmet needs of parents of children with sickle cell anemia. *Proceedings of the First National Symposium on Sickle Cell Disease.* Washington, DC: National Institutes of Health.

Williams, I., Earles, A., & Pack, B. (1983). Psychological considerations in sickle cell disease. *Nursing Clinics of North America, 18*(1), 215–229.

6. Families and Post-Traumatic Stress Disorder

David Rosenthal, PhD
Associate Professor
Family Practice
University of Iowa
Iowa City, Iowa

Anne Sadler, RN, MS
Doctoral Student
Counselor Education
University of Iowa
Iowa City, Iowa

Warren Edwards, PhD
Chief, Psychology Service
V.A. Medical Center
Iowa City, Iowa

I have spent my adult life in a state of premature death embrace, like watching a suspense movie when you know the ending. (Hittel, 1986, p. 8)

Individuals who have experienced a threat of annihilation may develop post-traumatic stress disorder (PTSD). Although symptoms of severe psychological trauma have been recognized for more than 200 years, there is as yet no definitive characterization of PTSD, its course, or its treatment. In addition to traditionally recognized stressor events such as war, accidents, and natural disasters, events such as incest, rape, crime victimization, terrorism, and violent deaths of loved ones are currently considered possible causes of PTSD.

Catastrophe victims experience a loss of equilibrium in their daily functioning. Aftermath perceptions are marked by a sense of insecurity, a pervasive sense of danger, and self-questioning. These are believed to result from the collapse of three assumptions that most people share: (1) the perception of personal invulnerability, (2) a belief in the world as a meaningful and comprehensible place, and (3) a positive self-view (Janoff-Bulman, 1985). Therefore, catastrophe victimizes not only the actual survivor, but also family members who witness the trauma or its result, or who are vicariously exposed to the trauma through the symptoms and abreactions of the victim.

81

HISTORICAL CONSIDERATIONS

Symptoms similar to those associated with PTSD were noted as early as 1623 when Shakespeare's Lady Percy observed that her warrior husband Hotspur experienced recurrent dreams of war (Davidson & Baum, 1985). Many trauma-induced symptoms were first observed in the study of soldiers and war. Civil War soldiers were said to be shell-shocked or brain-damaged as a result of artillery fire blasts; their clinical symptoms included paralysis, mutism, blindness, anxiety, irritability, tremors, nightmares, insomnia, and startle reactions (Ettedgni & Bridges, 1985). Bitter debates began to arise in medical circles as to whether symptoms that appeared long after travel and war injuries resulted from obscure injuries to the brain or reflected a "nervous condition" (Kolb, 1984).

After railway travel became popular in the 19th century, trauma-induced symptoms were observed in the survivors of train accidents. Erichsen (1882) was one of the first physicians to describe "railway spine," or "concussion of the spine," a trauma-induced lesion of the spinal cord or brain that produced symptoms similar to those of PTSD. Symptoms of railway spine, which was thought to be due to changes in the molecular structure of the cord, might not appear for years following the injury. This theory was congruent with the prevailing attitude that emotional disturbances had an organic etiology (Davidson & Baum, 1985). Page (1885) attempted to bridge the emotional-organic gap by suggesting that some cases could be ascribed primarily to emotional causes and some primarily to organic causes. He used the term *nervous shock* to describe symptoms in patients with no evident organic injury from traumatic accidents (Davidson & Baum, 1985).

Attention shifted away from these disorders until World War I. At that time, Freud developed psychoanalytic theory, changing the view of trauma and its effects. Freud believed that a traumatic neurosis arose when stressful stimuli overwhelmed an individual's ego defenses, either because of the intensity of the stimuli or because of a psychic "weakness" in the individual. As Freud described them, symptoms of a traumatic neurosis included a blocking or decrease in ego functions; sleep problems and/or catastrophic dreams; uncontrollable emotions, such as anxiety and anger; and psychoneurotic secondary complications (Fenichel, 1945).

Freud discussed the traumatic neuroses of war in terms of the "war superego" and the "peace superego." He felt that the war superego permitted the expression of forbidden impulses and led to a danger of breakdown because it freed the personality from the responsibility usually felt in peacetime (Fenichel, 1945). During World War I, attention was focused on shell shock or "traumatic neurosis," and Freud's theories received a great deal of support. Traumatized soldiers were felt to be detrimental to troop morale and were hurried into quick treatment so that they could return to the front for combat duty. This practice was usually unsuccessful, however, and most men with shell shock returned to hospitals and eventually to the Veteran's service (Rando, 1942).

Kardiner expanded Freud's concept of a traumatic neurosis into a traumatic neurosis of war (Kardiner, 1959; Rando, 1942). Symptoms resulted from conflict between the subject's relationship to his own resources and his relationship to the group, according to Kardiner. A distorted relationship greatly exaggerated the subject's sense of external danger, resulting in (1) altered self-concept in relation to the outer world, (2) the catastrophic dream, (3) startle pattern and irritability, (4) proclivity to explosive aggressive reaction, (5) decreased functioning level that includes such aspects of intelligence as cognition and perception, (6) hopelessness and fear of annihilation, and (7) a craving for compensation (Kardiner, 1959). For a brief time, an organic etiology was once again considered responsible for the aberrant phenomena. It was postulated that the concussion of artillery explosions produced microstructural lesions in the central nervous system. Large numbers of autopsies failed to uncover any evidence of organic changes, however, and psychoanalytic methods of explaining war neuroses were more fully embraced.

In World War II, traumatic war neuroses were called "combat neuroses," "combat stress," "gross stress reaction," and "operational fatigue" (Andreasen, 1980). The incidence of psychiatric casualties increased more than 300% from the World War I figure, and the symptoms were attributed to stress, fatigue, exposure to harsh environmental conditions, and extreme danger. In an effort to avoid evacuation, aggressive treatment strategies were used at the front; sodium thiopental (Pentothal) or hypnosis was frequently included in treatment. It was argued that the reactions occurred primarily in soldiers who were somehow psychologically unable to deal with stress (Davidson & Baum, 1985). At that time, the combat disorder was considered a transient state, and there was some debate as to whether "combat fatigue" and psychoneurosis were separate syndromes (Lewis & Engle, 1954).

A study done primarily with World War II veterans demonstrated the persistence of the stress reaction. The pulse and respiration rates, in combat veterans who were listening to recordings of combat sounds were significantly different from those in a control group (Dobbs & Wilson, 1960). This illustrated that stress reactions were not necessarily transient, as suggested by *DSM I*.

After the world wars, interest in stress reactions abated. Toward the end of the Vietnam War, interest began to increase, reaching a crescendo with the return of the hostages from Iran in 1980. Research and professional literature on PTSD with victims of natural disasters and catastrophic accidents, concentration camp survivors, ex-political prisoners, and Vietnam veterans has proliferated ever since.

DIAGNOSTIC CONSIDERATIONS

PTSD appeared as a diagnostic category for the first time in the American Psychiatric Association's third edition of the *Diagnostic and Statistical Manual of Mental Disorders (DSM III)*. It is one of the few disorders in the *DSM III* that focuses on etiology (Green, Wilson, & Lindy, 1985). There are five criteria listed in the *DSM III* as necessary for the diagnosis:

A. Existence of recognizable stressor that would evoke significant symptoms of distress in almost everyone.

B. Reexperiencing of the trauma as evidenced by at least one of the following:

   1. recurrent and intrusive recollections of the event
   2. recurrent dreams of the event
   3. sudden acting or feeling as if the traumatic event were reoccurring, because of an association with an environmental or ideational stimulus

C. Numbing of the responsiveness to or reduced involvement with the external world, beginning sometime after the trauma, as shown by at least one of the following:

   1. markedly diminished interest in one or more significant activities
   2. feeling of detachment or estrangement from others
   3. constricted affect

D. At least two of the following symptoms that were not present before the trauma:

   1. hyperalertness or exaggerated startle response
   2. sleep disturbance
   3. guilt about surviving when others have not, or about behavior required for survival
   4. memory impairment or trouble concentrating
   5. avoidance of activities that arouse recollection of the traumatic event

6. intensification of symptoms by exposure to events that symbolize or resemble the traumatic event (p. 238)

Individuals may develop PTSD at any age. Symptoms may begin immediately after the trauma or may remain latent for months or years. Those that
occur within 6 months of the trauma and do not last longer than 6 months are
considered acute and are likely to be resolved. Symptoms that do not appear
until at least 6 months after the trauma are considered delayed; if they continue for more than 6 months, they are considered chronic.

Kilpatrick, Veronen, and Best (1985) found that, irrespective of predisposi-
tion, the time at which symptoms first appear is the best predictor of long-term
chronic distress. If the initial traumatic stress immediately follows a catastrophe (6 to 21 days), the Horowitz model suggests that PTSD is a cyclical
illness with periods of quiescence, or avoidance, and periods of intrusion.
Intrusions occur when defenses are low. The episodic nature of PTSD may be
related to the anniversary of specific events, environmental reminders of the
experience, or a symptomatically differential response to treatment (Green,
1985). Reactions may vary widely and are dependent on circumstances such as
the duration of the trauma, the age of the victim, and the cause of the
catastrophe (i.e., man-made or an act of nature). Natural disasters appear to
cause PTSD less frequently than do man-made disasters, possibly because
intact support systems are struck simultaneously in a natural disaster and there
is no blaming a single victim (Figley, 1985).

General practitioners are least likely to detect PTSD. Even experienced
psychiatrists have difficulty with the diagnosis, as chronic PTSD is often
observed in the context of other Axis I (primary diagnosis) disorders as well as
some aspects of Axis II (personality trait) disorders (Green et al., 1985;
McFarlane, 1986). Symptoms are sometimes confused with those of other
clinical conditions. For example, intrusive images may be mistaken for hallu-
cinations in schizophrenia; reenactments may be interpreted as acting out
behavior in personality disorders (Green, 1985). Generalized anxiety disorders, major affective disorders, and paranoid disorders may also mask PTSD.

In a recent systematic review of symptoms, the mental health staff of the
Veterans Administration agreed that the following symptoms, listed in
decreasing order of importance, have the greatest value in the differential
diagnosis of PTSD (Keane & Penk, 1986):

1. recurrent dreams of the event
2. startle responses
3. acting or feeling as if the event were recurring
4. distressing memories of the death of another
5. hypervigilance

6. efforts to avoid thoughts of a troublesome event
7. intensification of symptoms when exposed to cause
8. difficulty feeling close
9. fear of losing control

Although PTSD was the only description given the Veterans Administration clinicians asked to select symptoms most characteristic of the illness, their answers strongly suggest that their frame of reference was combat-related stress disorder.

A profound problem in the diagnosis and treatment of PTSD is the tendency of these patients to go to considerable lengths (e.g., by self-medication with alcohol or drugs) to remove their painful and intrusive thoughts from awareness. Moreover, little is known as to whether people who are aware of their PTSD symptoms see themselves as ill and in need of treatment. Some sociologists consider such symptoms indicative of problems with living that are very common after natural disasters, rather than indicative of a disorder (McFarlane, 1986). Such "hair-splitting" becomes academic, however, in view of the readily apparent distress of the victims.

ASPECTS OF CATASTROPHE

Catastrophe is an extraordinary event that makes its victims feel out of control, helpless, frightened, and overwhelmed. It is likely to leave a lasting impression that they would prefer to forget (Figley, 1985). Figley and McCubbin (1983) differentiated the normative stressors of life from catastrophic stressors. Green, Wilson, and Lindy (1985) speculate that (1) the role of the survivor in catastrophe and (2) the degree of life threat, warning, displacement, and exposure to the grotesque have the most profound effect on survivor adjustment. Wilson, Smith, and Johnson (1985) indicated that many of the parameters of catastrophic events may serve as variables that determine individual PTSD responses.

Little or No Time to Prepare. The more rapid the onset of trauma, the greater the consequences of "one-trial learning." The victim is prevented from planning or rehearsing survival strategy. Rapid onset of trauma is likely to be associated with learned helplessness, a sense of external control, and internal anxiety (Figley & McCubbin, 1983; Wilson et al., 1985).

Few Sources of Guidance. Victims and families who must cope with abandonment, death, terrorism, and other catastrophes have few resources in literature or media that provide education or support (Figley & McCubbin, 1983).

Interminable Time in Crisis. Catastrophe may last from hours to years. As every person has a point of vulnerability that will be reached if the trauma persists long enough, the duration of a catastrophe can be expected to correlate strongly with the severity of PTSD symptoms, such as psychic numbing, intrusive imagery, memory impairment, physical health problems, and dissociative reactions (Figley & McCubbin, 1983; Wilson et al., 1985). Niederland (1968) described the "living corpse appearance" of concentration camp survivors, noting that prolonged confrontation with death had given them a macabre, shadowy, or ghostlike imprint.

Lack of Control/Helplessness. Victims caught in catastrophic situations are usually powerless to modulate the sources of stress (Figley & McCubbin, 1983). Eighty-eight percent of rape victims described themselves as helpless in the situation (Kilpatrick, 1985). Victims of all types of catastrophes continue to perceive themselves as helpless after the stressor event (Danieli, 1985). They come to believe that their destiny is shaped by external forces over which they have little or no control. They see the world as a hostile and threatening place that can cause them further suffering; they ultimately develop a learned helplessness, depression, isolation, and anxiety associated with fear of recurrent trauma (Wilson et al., 1985).

Sense of Loss/Bereavement. Loss can involve death, roles, skills, responsibility, innocence, time, fantasy, or goals. Associated PTSD symptoms often include depression, grief, and rage at the source (Figley & McCubbin, 1983; Wilson et al., 1985). In a crisis, such as war, the process of mourning is greatly curtailed. Much of what passes as cynicism or apathy is really a surfeit of bereavement (Shapiro, 1978).

Disruption and Destruction. Catastrophe often leaves far-reaching and permanent change. Destruction of the victim's entire life style is possible (Figley & McCubbin, 1983). At the Buffalo Creek flood disaster, for example, people who lost their homes and first-degree relatives appeared to be most at risk of pathological bereavement; with total destruction of property, not even a single photograph or memento of the dead person remained (McFarlane, 1986).

Dangerousness—Degree of Life Threat. The threat of physical harm or death elicits the most intense of human emotion. The greater the degree of life threat, the more likely the fear of annihilation and death. The autonomic nervous system is likely to respond with excessive anxiety, hyperalertness, and hypervigilance, as well as intrusive imagery (Figley & McCubbin, 1983; Wilson, et al., 1985).

Exposure to Death and Destruction. Mere exposure to death, dying, and destruction can precipitate PTSD. The greater the exposure of catastrophic events, the more likely the survivor will develop intrusive imagery, isolation, survivor guilt, psychic numbing, and changes in personality and values (Wilson et al., 1985). Medical personnel in Vietnam developed feelings of pervasive helplessness, inadequacy, isolation, and anger because of the futility of their efforts to deal with overwhelming human destruction, for example (Dewane, 1984).

Degree of Moral Conflict Inherent in the Situation. Many traumatic situations place the victim into moral conflict regarding the value of life, family, property, friends, and community. Moral conflict can contribute to moral and survivor guilt, as well as to value changes (Figley & McCubbin, 1983; Wilson et al., 1985). The Vietnam veteran, for example, was forced to confront complex moral issues at a developmental stage in life when few people have developed a coherent personal values code (Harrington & Jay, 1982).

Role of the Victim in the Trauma. In some traumatic situations, individuals react passively to the stressors; in other cases (e.g., combat), individuals act as agents who contribute to the trauma. Victims are likely to have strong feelings about what they did or did not do. A passive reaction role may cause the victim to feel anxiety and rage. The agent role may cause guilt, self-recrimination, and isolation (Wilson et al., 1985).

Proportion of the Community That the Trauma Effects. A widespread destruction of homes and property gives its victims a sense of shared fate; however, it produces an immediate change in the survivors' sense of belonging to a stable social order (Wilson et al., 1985). The Beverly Hills Supper Club fire disaster was sudden, but the duration was short and the community was not destroyed; the fire survivors could return to intact homes and support systems. Two years after the fire, survivors were normal in terms of psychopathology, but this was not the case for survivors of the Buffalo Creek flood (Green, Grace, Lindy, Titchener, & Lindy, 1983).

IMPACT ON FAMILIES

Coping methods of catastrophe victims and their families show more similarities than differences. It is vital to recognize that all family members are affected by a catastrophic life event, even when they have not simultaneously experienced the event. Family members also lose their assumptions of personal invulnerability, their belief in the world as a meaningful place, and their positive self-views. In addition, families vicariously experience the trauma and psychic pain of the survivor. Figley (1985) called this process a chiasmal effect, or an "infection" of the family with trauma. He noted that this transmission of behaviors has been widely reported in the literature under the terms *symbiosis, identification, sympathy, couvade, secondary victimization, indirect victimization,* and *vicarious victimization.* The greater the victim distress, the greater the supporter distress.

Family members are further affected by the victim's reconstruction of values and methods of coping. If the family system has previously functioned in a positive, adaptive manner, the prognosis for recovery of both victim and family is good. Vietnam veterans from unusually stable family backgrounds were found to have a higher stressor tolerance than did those from average families; those who returned to close-knit families showed significantly fewer symptoms than did those with little or poor family supports (Egendorf, Kadushin, Laufer, Rothbart, & Sloan, 1981).

When the trauma comes from within the family, all family members are directly affected. Those families in which there has been alcoholism, physical abuse or sexual abuse tend to perpetuate dysfunction, as they are relatively disorganized. It is especially traumatizing that the source of comfort and support is simultaneously the source of discomfort and pain (Figley & McCubbin, 1983). Children who grow up in such a family have no perspective, language, or experience that allows them to stand outside these relational imbalances and to develop a healthy psychological outlook, a positive sense of self, or the ability to maintain positive relationships (Gelinas, 1983). Victims of intrafamilial abuse do, however, adopt the same basic cognitive processes that victims of other catastrophes adopt (i.e., stress, denial, numbing, active-passive role, coping, adjustment, healing recapitulation; Figley, 1985).

Families of survivors of either extra- or intrafamilial trauma may develop the following characteristics:

1. PTSD symptoms
2. boundary distortions of intimacy and separation (enmeshment)
3. somatization of rage and grief
4. family rule of fear and mistrust of the outside world (closed family boundaries)
5. parentification of children
6. patronization of victim
7. distraction from the stressful event (encouraged avoidance)
8. ambivalent feelings toward the victim because of the stigma (sexual or moral) of the event or because of what the victim did or did not do to survive
9. substance abuse
10. profound need for social support, but inability to encourage healthy, positive interventions
11. feelings of unworthiness or guilt
12. self-destructive behavior (suicide, self-biting, burning)

13. investment of self-esteem in the ability to influence and control the behavior of self and others
14. efforts to meet others' needs at the expense of personal needs
15. need to be in control
16. abusive language
17. failure of family to allow members to pass through developmental stages
18. overreactions to stress of daily living
19. unreasoning prejudices (political, racial, gender)

The specific characteristics and the degree of their intensity vary among families.

TREATMENT

The difficulties of working with people who suffer from PTSD have been clearly documented. Horowitz and Solomon (1978) focused on (1) distrust, (2) hostile impulses, (3) a fear of committing aggressive acts, and (4) a fear of authority figures as significant barriers that must be overcome in treatment. Walker and Nash (1981) listed four characteristics of the Vietnam combat veteran that they believed to have an effect on treatment: (1) the feeling of being scapegoated, (2) psychic numbing or learning to suppress feelings, (3) a sense of alienation, and (4) guilt over having maimed and killed other human beings.

Initially, regardless of the therapeutic approach selected, the therapist must focus on joining with the client (Minuchin & Fishman, 1981). The therapist must realize that clients with PTSD, particularly veterans, may be reluctant to talk; at the same time, the therapist must offer them the opportunity to discuss their experiences (Egendorf, 1978). A strong, trustful therapist-client alliance is essential if clients are to feel comfortable discussing a personally traumatic event. The therapist should be aware, however, that the intensity of a client's memories may make the therapist feel vulnerable to his or her own feelings about catastrophe and attitudes about killing (Haley, 1985; Janoff-Bulman, 1985).

According to Walker and Nash (1981), neither psychoanalytic nor cognitive therapy is effective for Vietnam combat veterans. They argue that unless veterans have absolute trust in the therapist, a somewhat inactive therapy such as psychoanalysis may make them more vulnerable to "paranoid ideation." Although a more active approach, cognitive therapy may exacerbate their feelings of being alienated and misunderstood. Brende (1981) suggested that an effective approach should help the individual to integrate any split off traumatic experiences. He suggested that a reenactment of these events in the present can be a first step in the process of integration.

Overall, the needs of individuals with PTSD can be met in a multimodal fashion. Certain issues related to the individual victims and their functioning can be treated best in a group setting. A safe group that focuses on building relationships can be helpful to many of these individuals, who use a variety of behaviors to keep from getting close to others and, thus, avoid the risk of getting hurt. In addition, resistance and mistrust can be neutralized in a group of people who have had similar experiences. Watching others overcome their own problems in a group setting (e.g., rap groups for Vietnam veterans) can also be therapeutic (Walker & Nash, 1981).

An adjunct to the group work in many cases should be family treatment, as living with an individual who has PTSD affects spouses (Palmer & Harris, 1983) and children (Rosenheck, 1986). For example, many wives of veterans feel excluded from a significant part of their husband's life, a part that continues to influence their husband's behavior. When they see their husband becoming depressed, they may try to help him feel better. Rejection of their attempts at help and intimacy may result in resentment, anger, and a distancing in the marital relationship. According to Palmer and Harris (1983), many of these women feel "trapped and defeated, unable to deal effectively with their anger" and begin to develop symptoms of their own. More specifically, many complain of anxiety, social isolation, hopelessness, and depression.

Rosenheck (1986) commented that children of Vietnam veterans who are close to their father seem to absorb some of their father's pain and carry it into their own adult lives, where it has an impact on their choice of marital partner, career, and lifestyle. In one case, a 10-year-old boy described himself "as getting all tense and confused" (p. 258) when things go berserk at home, and it became evident that he had developed numerous fears and fantasies from these experiences (Rosenheck & Nathan, 1985). Many of these feelings appeared to mimic the kinds of symptoms that his father experienced with PTSD.

When initiating treatment for a family that has a member with PTSD, the therapist should focus on whatever issues the family raises. Some therapists push the treatment to focus on the traumatic event prematurely. Many people and their families have learned not to share emotions, however, and the therapist should join with the family and make them feel comfortable talking about their lives before trying to focus on the unspoken. To shift the focus onto another problem immediately may only increase the victim's mistrust and result in premature termination of therapy.

Following the joining stages of family therapy, the therapist should alleviate the family's initial concern and only then move toward issues related to the traumatic event. Figley (1985) pointed out that families can be helpful by

"1) detecting traumatic stress, 2) confronting the trauma, 3) urging the recapitulation of the catastrophe, and 4) facilitating resolution of the trauma-inducing conflicts" (p. 408). In addition, he argued that "reconsideration" is a necessary step in the recovery process. It is not always a necessary step, however. Therapists do not need to replicate the power struggle that may already exist in the family by pushing for full disclosure. Some spouses have continually urged disclosure and have felt ineffective and helpless when it did not occur. Thus, the maintenance of the secret may become more important in the family dance than is the secret itself.

If the individual is using the group experience to discuss the traumatic events, it may not be necessary for him or her to discuss the events in detail with the family. Disclosure does not always result in behavior change, and establishing disclosure as the only therapeutic goal may limit therapeutic options. The therapist must not only be aware that people change for different reasons, but also be flexible enough to find those reasons (Ault-Riché & Rosenthal, in press).

> One couple never discussed the traumatic experience, but worked instead on family issues. The veteran spent a few group sessions reliving his previous war experience, and the entire family noticed the impact that the group disclosures had on their relationship. In a later family session, the veteran said he was still not prepared to discuss his war experience with his family, but felt that disclosure in the group had helped. The family later reported that things had improved at home.

Another couple never discussed the traumatic event, but felt that they had learned new coping skills while discussing their relationship. A third family changed when a Vietnam focus was reframed as a fear of taking risks and failing. In each case, the therapist remained flexible enough to look for the most efficient way to bring about change.

Adjunctive educational methods may be used to instruct family members about PTSD and, in the case of Vietnam veterans, about the nature of the combat conditions in the Vietnam war. It has been suggested that psycho-educational methods of treatment, combined with other forms of therapy, may help entire families to cope with difficult situations (Anderson, Griffin, Rossi, Pagonis, Holder, & Treiber, 1986). These approaches can focus on the etiology of the problem and on positive responses. Quite often, when given additional information, family members feel less helpless in their interactions with the symptom bearer and less anxious that they will make the situation worse.

REFERENCES

American Psychiatric Association. (1980). *Diagnostic and Statistical Manual,* (3rd ed.). Washington, DC: Author.

Anderson, C.M., Griffin, S., Rossi A., Pagonis, J., Holder, D.P., & Treiber, R. (June 1986). A comparative study of the impact of education vs. process groups for families of patients with affective disorders. *Family Process, 25* (2), 185–206.

Andreasen, N.C. (1980). Post-traumatic stress disorder. In A.M. Freedman, H.I. Kaplan, & B.J. Saddock (Eds.), *Comprehensive textbook of psychiatry: III* (pp. 1517–1525). Baltimore: Williams & Wilkins.

Ault-Riché, M., & Rosenthal, D.M. (in press). *Family therapy for a new age.* Englewood Cliffs, NJ: Prentice-Hall.

Brende, J.O. (1981). Combined individual and group therapy for Vietnam veterans. *International Journal of Group Psychotherapy, 31*(3), 367–377.

Bulman, R., & Wortman, C.B. (1977). Attributions of blame and coping in the "real world": Severe accident victims react to their lot. *Journal of Personality and Social Psychology, 35,* 351 363.

Danieli, Y. (1985). The treatment and prevention of long-term effects and intergenerational transmission of victimization: A lesson from Holocaust survivors and their children. In C.R. Figey (Ed.), *Trauma and its wake: The study and treatment of post-traumatic stress disorder* (pp. 295–313). New York: Brunner/Mazel.

Davidson, L.M., & Baum, A. (1985). Implications of post-traumatic stress for social psychology. In S. Oskamp (Ed.), *International conflict and national public policy issues: Applied social psychology annual 6* (pp. 207–232). Beverly Hills, CA: Sage Publications.

Dewane, C.J. (December 1984). Posttraumatic stress disorder in medical personnel in Vietnam. *Hospital and Community Psychiatry, 35*(12), 1232–1234.

Dobbs, D., & Wilson, W.P. (1960). Observations on persistence of war neurosis. *Disease of the Nervous System, 21,* 686–691.

Egendorf, A., Kadushin, C., Laufer R.S., Rothbart, G., & Sloan, L. (1981). Summary of findings. In *Legacies of Vietnam: Comparative adjustment of veterans and their peers,* vol. 2. Washington, DC: Government Printing Office.

Egendorf, F.A. (1978). Psychotherapy with Vietnam veterans: Observations and suggestions. In C. Figley (Ed.), *Stress disorders among Vietnam veterans.* New York: Brunner/Mazel.

Erichsen, J.A. (1882). *On concussion of the spine: Nervous shock and other obscure injuries of the nervous system in their clinical and medico-legal aspect.* London: Longmans, Green, & Company, pp. 20–29.

Ettedgni, E., & Bridges, M. (1985). Post-traumatic shock disorder. *Psychiatric Clinics of North America, 8*(1), 89–103.

Fenichel, O. (1945). *The traumatic neuroses.* New York: W.W. Norton.

Figley, C.F. (1985). *Trauma and its wake: The study and treatment of posttraumatic stress disorder.* New York: Brunner/Mazel.

Figley, C.R., & McCubbin, H.I. (1983). *Stress and the family* (Vol. 3). New York: Brunner/Mazel.

Gelinas, D.J. (1983). The persisting negative effects of incest. *Psychiatry, 46,* 312–332.

Green, B.L., Grace, M.C., Lindy, J.C., Titchener, J.L., & Lindy, J.G. (1983). Levels of functional impairment following a civilian disaster: The Beverly Hills Supper Club Fire. *Journal of Consulting and Clinical Psychology, 51*(4), 573–580.

Green, B.L., Lindy, J.D., & Grace, M.C. (1985). Post-traumatic stress disorder: Toward DSM-IV. *The Journal of Nervous and Mental Disorders, 173*(7), 406–411.

Green, B.L., Wilson, J.P., & Lindy, J.D. (1985). Conceptualizing post-traumatic stress disorder: A psychosocial framework. In C.R. Figley (Ed.), *Trauma and its wake: The study and treatment of post-traumatic stress disorder* (pp. 53–72). New York: Brunner/Mazel.

Haley, S.A. (1985). Some of my best friends are dead: Treatment of the post-traumatic stress disorder patient and his family. *Family Systems Medicine, 3*(1), 17–26.

Harrington, D.S., & Jay, J.A. (1982, May-June). Beyond the family: Value issues in the treatment of Vietnam veterans. *Family Therapy Networker*, pp. 13–15, 44–45.

Hittel, R. (1986). "Premature death embrace" plagues combat veteran. *Voice, 7*(8), 8–9.

Horowitz, M., Solomon, G. (1978). Delayed stress response syndromes in Vietnam veterans. In C.R. Figley (Ed.), *Stress disorders among Vietnam veterans* (pp. 67–80). New York: Brunner/Mazel.

Janoff-Bulman, R. (1985). The aftermath of victimization: Rebuilding shattered assumptions. In C.R. Figley (Ed.), *Trauma and its wake: The study and treatment of post-traumatic stress disorder* (pp. 15–36). New York: Brunner/Mazel.

Kardiner, A. (1959). Traumatic neuroses of war. In S. Arieti (Ed.), *American Handbook of Psychiatry* (Vol. 1, pp. 245–247). New York: Basic Books.

Keane, T., & Penk, W.E. (1986, July 19). Systematic internal review: Diagnostic concordance on differential diagnostic signs between post-traumatic stress and major depressive disorders for VAMC psychology and psychiatry outpatient staff. *Veteran Administration Memorandum.*

Kilpatrick, D.G., Veronen, L.J., & Best, C.L. (1985). Factors predicting psychological distress among rape victims. In C.R. Figley (Ed.), *Trauma and its wake: The study and treatment of post-traumatic stress disorder* (pp. 113–141). New York: Brunner/Mazel.

Kolb, L.C. (1984). The post-traumatic stress disorders of combat: A subgroup with a conditioned emotional response. *Military Medicine, 149*(3), 237–243.

Lewis, N., & Engle, B. (1954). *Wartime psychiatry.* New York: Oxford University Press, pp. 86–94.

McFarlane, M.B. (1986). Post-traumatic morbidity of a disaster: A study of cases presenting for psychiatric treatment. *The Journal of Nervous and Mental Disease, 174*(1), 4–14.

Minuchin, S., & Fishman, H.C. (1981). *Family therapy techniques.* Cambridge: Harvard University Press.

Niederland, W.G. (1968). Clinical observations of the "survivor syndrome." *International Journal of Psychoanalysis, 49,* 313–315.

Page, H.D. (1885). *Injuries of the spine and spinal cord without apparent mechanical lesion.* London: Churchill, pp. 26–42.

Palmer, S., & Harris, M. (1983). Supportive group therapy for women partners of Vietnam veterans. *The Family Therapist, 4*(2), 3–11.

Rando, S. (1942). Pathodynamics and treatment of traumatic war neurosis (tramatophobia). *Psychosomatic Medicine, 4,* 362–368.

Rosenheck, R. (1986). Impact of post-traumatic stress disorder of World War II on the next generation. *The Journal of Nervous and Mental Disease, 174*(6), 319–327.

Rosenheck, R., & Nathan, P. (1985). Secondary traumatization in children of Vietnam veterans. *Hospital and Community Psychiatry, 36*(5), 538–539.

Shapiro, R.B. (1978). Working through the war with Vietnam vets. *Group, 2*(3), 156–183.

Walker, J.I., & Nash, J.L. (1981). Group therapy in the treatment of Vietnam combat veterans. *International Journal of Group Psychotherapy, 31*(3), 379–389.

Wilson, J.P., Smith, W.K., & Johnson, S.K. (1985). A comparative analysis of PTSD among various survivor groups. In C.R. Figley (Ed.), *Trauma and its wake: The study and treatment of post-traumatic stress disorder* (pp. 142–172). New York: Brunner/Mazel.

7. Farm Families

Elizabeth Loeb, MD
Assistant Professor
Family Practice
University of Iowa
Iowa City, Iowa

Joanne Dvorak, MSW
Program Director
Farmers Helping Farmers
Family Service Agency
Cedar Rapids, Iowa

F *arming.* In the past, this word brought to mind pastoral scenes, fresh air, clean living, and a stable family life with men and women in traditional roles. In recent years, however, this concept has been altered by plummeting land prices, record farm debts, and bankruptcies that threaten the very fabric of the American farm community to a degree unprecedented since the Great Depression of the 1930s. Today's farmer must be knowledgeable in veterinary medicine, mechanics, finance, economics, construction, and domestic and foreign government policy in order to be competitive in the world marketplace. Farmers must hire others to do their work in areas where they themselves lack expertise, which cuts into profit margins and possibly jeopardizes the solvency of the farm.

This situation creates a high level of stress in the majority of today's farm families, and health professionals must be aware of this stress in order to deal effectively with the farm family as a unit. Furthermore, health professionals must be well versed in farm family dynamics before they can understand the impact of external factors on those dynamics. They must realize that the farm marriage has evolved into more of a partnership in the farm operation, although the farm husband often makes final business decisions.

ECONOMICS OF FARMING

The Homestead Act of May 20, 1862, offered enterprising pioneers a chance to obtain a farm if they had the stamina and the courage to farm the land for 5 years to obtain legal ownership of the land. These farmers were generally self-sufficient, growing most of what they needed on the farm and earning only a little cash to purchase the supplies that they could not produce themselves. Government policies did not make or break these farmers; the rigors of farming did. Children (generally sons) who wanted to become farmers either inherited land or paid for it from family loans or personal savings. Gradually, however, commercial loans became the predominant means of purchasing a farm, especially from 1961 to 1976. This shift in financing probably resulted from the increased cost; the initial investment in land and buildings *alone* increased from $20,504 in 1920 to $297,573 in 1985 (Dorner & Marquardt, 1978; Iowa Farm Bureau Federation, 1985).

Farmland itself increased in price most rapidly during the 1970s, with a 55% increase in value between 1977 and 1981 (Hines, Green, & Petrulis, 1985). The average price of an acre of Iowa farmland peaked at approximately $2,100 in 1981 and plummeted to $948 by 1985 (Muhm, 1986). Because the land accounts for three-fourths of a farm's assets, this wild fluctuation in land prices was extremely damaging, especially to farmers aged 45 or younger who began farming in the 1970s and to older farmers who had expanded their operations in the 1970s to provide income and work for two generations of the family. This was the most costly time to invest in new land, equipment, etc., and it was primarily these two groups who expanded farm operations. Land that had been used as collateral for further loans obtained for planting, new buildings, or new farm machinery suddenly dwindled in value, creating high debt:asset ratios (Heffernan & Heffernan, 1985). In 1985, 7.3% of U.S. farmers had a debt:asset ratio of more than 70% (7 dollars owed to the lending institutions for every 10 dollars of assets) near the point of insolvency (Hines et al., 1985).

Today's farmers have become increasingly specialized, are more dependent on capital for their operations, and must farm more acres to pay for the costs of farming. Their well-being is also more vulnerable to government policies and worldwide economics. In the 1970s, there was a fivefold increase in exports, the value of the dollar was generally low, and interest rates were low. Farmers expanded operations to meet foreign demands. The worldwide recession of the early 1980s, the increase in interest rates, the decline of commodity prices, a 13% decrease in exports, and the Russian grain embargo all combined to hurt farmers (Hines et al., 1985).

Farm husbands and farm wives have had to turn increasingly to off-farm jobs in order to keep their farms solvent. Farm operators in the Midwest may find it difficult to obtain off-farm employment, however, because the farm crisis has adverse effects on the agriculturally based industries of that region. Employment statistics may not indicate the actual number of farmers who hold multiple jobs, as employment statistics are often based on the job that produces the most income and farming may produce less income than does the off-farm job. In areas such as the Midwest, women find jobs more readily, because they traditionally are employed in lower paying, nonadvancing service-related areas that are more recession-proof than are agriculturally related industries (DeAre & Kalbacher, 1985). The multiple jobs can be an additional source of stress to farmers and their families, who must now work longer hours to remain solvent.

THE FARM FAMILY

While city dwellers usually have a clear separation of the workplace from home life and household tasks, farm families often integrate farm chores and household work. Furthermore, the roles of the farm family are not as well defined as those of city dwellers. Farm families may consist of one to three generations working together. There may be a formal or legal definition of the farm roles or tasks of different family members, which fosters mutual dependence. Legal contracts that define farm roles may also hamper what was previously an open and democratic decision-making process, especially when documents delineate intergenerational transfers and the role changes between farmers and their children.

Because the family is so critical to the survival of a farm, the family unit tolerates more stress before divorcing or breaking a legal contract than does a nonfarm family (Coward & Smith, 1981). Divorce rates among farm couples are always lower than are those among nonfarm couples, partly because of the importance of the family unit to the welfare of the farm and partly because of farmers' tendency to have more conservative views toward life styles and family life (*Report on Lifestyles/Personal Health in Different Occupations, 1979*). In 1984, the percentages of divorced farmers was 1.6%, compared to 8% of nonfarm dwellers; the percentage of separated farmers was 0.5%, compared to 2.8% (De Are & Kalbacher, 1985). The present farm crisis may change the divorce statistics, as some families now going through the stress of farm foreclosure may not be able to salvage their marriage when the process has been completed. One study of families that had owned farms showed a 9.5% divorce rate after foreclosure (Heffernan & Heffernan, 1985).

Working hours vary greatly on a farm, depending on the season. Family members may work 16- to 18-hour days with no weekends off during planting and harvesting season and then have little work to do in winter unless they have a large number of livestock or an off-farm job. Work often becomes routine and monotonous (Coward & Smith, 1981), and farmers may be forced to work even longer hours if bad weather is expected. Dealing with fluctuating market prices and government policies that adversely affect the farmer adds more stress.

Farm families may make material sacrifices for decades for the collective good of the farm; for example, they may postpone remodeling their home in order to make structural improvements in farm buildings. Families feel tied to the farm and may go years without vacationing or spending a night off the farm (Kohl, 1976).

Because of their ties to the farm's work demands, farm families are together both in work and in leisure. They may decrease the tension of being together for prolonged periods of time by decreasing the amount of contact that they have with each other inside the home or by doing more outside the home. If they are used to being together in the outdoors, they may note an increase in tension when they are confined to smaller spaces, such as during adverse weather conditions (Rosenblatt & Anderson, 1981).

The Farm Husband

Farms are usually passed down to sons, less often to daughters or sons-in-law. A son-in-law usually must have farm work experience before taking over management of the farm.

Early in his career, the farmer is likely to have an off-farm job to earn money for the purchase of the farm (Wilkening & Ahrens, 1979). Moreover, the father or son is likely to work off the farm during generational transfers (Dorner & Marquardt, 1979). More than 50% of farmers with a gross income less than $10,000 need to work off the farm in order to pay all the bills (Wilkening & Ahrens, 1979). Working fewer than 100 days off the farm produces less conflict for the farmer (Kada, 1978), but may not be possible if the farmer does not inherit land and must generate capital in order to purchase the farm. The full-time off-farm job, in addition to the farm demands, add up to long hours, fatigue, and physical stress.

If a man is farming with his father and/or brothers, the difficulty of defining the work roles and the decision-making power of various family members may increase family stress. An authoritarian style of operation on the part of the father may cause conflict within the son's nuclear family, as there is often no opportunity for extended family input and communication. The son may be unable to find a second job to provide income to save the farm (Fuson, 1986). The son and his nuclear family are likely to be guilt-ridden if it appears that they will lose a farm that has been in the family for generations and, thus, displace an elderly parent or dash a son's dream of farming.

The older farmer may be reluctant to retire, as farming is a way of life he has known since childhood. Thus, he may turn over full responsibility to a frustrated son only gradually unless there is a clear understanding between them or unless the older farmer dies or becomes severely ill. The farm and its demands have structured the farmer's time for years; having had little time to develop hobbies, he may not know how to redirect energy and face retirement. If the farmer does retire, his wife often continues to exclude him from traditional household tasks, thus making the transition to retirement more difficult for both of them (Kohl, 1976). In addition, the wife may become impatient with her husband if he relies on her to structure his time, as this is another burden for her.

The Farm Wife

Traditionally, farm wives have assumed the multiple roles of taking care of husband, children, and aged parents; housework; preparing meals; gardening; possibly sewing clothes; and working outside the home. In smaller farms, two-thirds of farm wives have equal or major responsibility for recordkeeping and paying bills. The wife's involvement in farm chores varies with the ages of her children, with the peak involvement occurring when her children are between 6 and 12 years old. The focus on child care begins to decrease as the children reach adolescence and are able to assist with chores themselves (Wilkening & Ahrens, 1979). The farm wife's dominant role in a farming enterprise and in her relationship with her spouse often changes during intergenerational farm transfer. She may reluctantly relinquish former tasks to growing children and, as a consequence, have decreased contact with her spouse.

The fertility of farm women has been higher than that of nonfarm women (2.1 children vs. 1.8 children in 1984), although the gap is narrowing (DeAre & Kalbacher, 1985). This prolongs the period during which the farm wife's primary responsibility is child care and intensifies a feeling of isolation that already exists. She may also feel that she is not contributing to the farm if taking care of small children prevents her from "choring."

An early study of farm life indicated that the farm wife can have either a positive or a negative effect on farming, depending on whether she is supportive of her husband or is in direct conflict with him (Beers, 1935). It appears, however, that her personal satisfaction with the farm operation is related to the family's standard of living and level of income (Bharadwaj & Wilkening, 1974). The wife's satisfaction with the farm may also be directly associated with the degree of her voluntary involvement in the farm operation. The farm wife may feel that she is contributing more to the farm if she can drive a tractor in the fields.

In a preliminary research study, farm women reported their primary role to be that of supporter to husband and children. In the two-generation farm operation, the mothers-in-law reported few changes in their role, task, or responsibilities, and they felt comfortable with this. These women expressed concern, however, that they would be caught in the middle of family and farm conflictual situations. They also worried about showing favoritism.

Because farm wives often manage farm/family finances, they are well aware of fluctuating cash flows that may interfere with family needs (Hedlund & Berkowitz, 1979). When there is a negative cash flow, such as when income tax or loan payments are due, they are still faced with the reality of monthly telephone, electricity, and food bills. These conditions often cause the family to delay visiting the dentist, purchasing eyeglasses, and meeting other family needs.

The farm crisis has forced more and more farm wives to seek off-farm employment in order to ensure a more stable cash flow for the family and to obtain health insurance benefits (Fuson, 1986). As an undesired consequence of off-farm employment, the farm wife may have less involvement in farm decisions (Wilkening & Ahrens, 1979). Paradoxically, the wife may want a larger decision-making role because of her new breadwinner status (Singleton, April 7, 1986). Off-farm employment adds to the family stress level, as there is a great deal of confusion about the wife's role. She is no longer a traditional farm wife, and she must either reassign some of her tasks to other family members or shoulder an additional burden. Finally, farm wives forced to take off-farm jobs because of large debts may be fearful that their depressed husbands will commit suicide while they are at work (Singleton, 1986).

Farm wives who *choose* a career and/or education may increase the stress on the farm family. The shift of the wife's focus off the farm mandates the reassignment of her responsibilities to others, and people in the farm community may not understand why she wants to make such a change. The farm crisis may alter these negative attitudes toward women returning to school, however, because such a step may increase their employability and their future wages. A new career not only benefits the family as a whole, but also infuses more money into local businesses.

Although the number of women who manage (i.e., make major business decisions and participate in field work) farms is low, the number has doubled in the last decade (Singleton, April 4, 1986; De Are & Kalbacher, 1985). These women are faced with the stresses of any of today's farm operators, as well as their other responsibilities (Singleton, April 4, 1986).

The Farm In-Law

As comparative outsiders to the farm, women who marry an adult son in multigenerational farm operation may face particular stress. If they have not been raised on a farm, tensions develop when they are perceived as lacking skills or interest in the farm. Even if they have been raised on a farm, their input may not be as highly regarded as that of their mother-in-law. The mother-in-law continues to be the matriarch of the farm family, leaving little or no power in the hands of her daughter-in-law or forcing her son to choose sides between his wife and his mother (Kohl, 1976). If he sides with his mother, he may maintain his level of power and decision making on the farm—but at the expense of his relationship with his wife. Siding with his wife may cause a rift between him and his parents, who are probably the main decision makers on the farm. Such a rift may lead to some type of "punishment" by his parents, such as exclusion from major business decisions on which he had been consulted on earlier occasions.

Young farm women, often daughters-in-law without farm backgrounds, have reported their primary duty as providing support to husband and children. Unlike their senior counterparts, however, young farm women report a real sense of changing roles for farm women and express confusion about their role in the farm operation. This role confusion creates a problem of "Who can I talk to?" "Am I crazy—farm wives have always been happy, secure people, so why do I feel so awful and scared?" One wife stated, "I'm trying to find my niche in the operation; my husband doesn't have time to teach me." Another stated, "I need to figure out what will make me happy and also help the farm operation—we need to talk about this." These women also report health problems, ranging from ulcers to headaches.

Farm Children

As they leave early childhood, farm children maintain contact with their parents through assigned daily chores. In the past, this has kept delinquency rates low in farm children (Kohl, 1976). A close work association can also increase tension, however, as the children *live* with their supervisors. Despite this, many farm children want to go into farming because they see their parents as positive role models (Bratton & Berkowitz, 1976; Stephens, 1979).

With the present farm crisis, farm children may express their stress through hostility and aggressiveness, alcohol abuse, and even promiscuity. School grades may drop, and children may demand more attention, develop sleep disturbances, cry more often, and become rebellious. Sons who have always wanted to farm may resent fathers who are in danger of losing farms that have been in the family for generations. Children may be denied necessary clothing, basic health care, and sufficient food because of the family's lack of money (Heffernan & Heffernan, 1985). In fact, the farm crisis may be harder on children than on parents, since outreach and support groups are usually oriented toward adults. Children who are experiencing the farm crisis suffer from fear of the unknown (e.g., "Will I graduate from my school, or will we have to move?"). Much of this is the result of limited communication with their parents, who are attempting to protect the children.

Adult Children

Often, older children leave the farm to establish their independence and acquire an area of expertise before returning to take part in the farm enterprise. Although raised to admire independence, they may be faced with a prolonged generational shift when their parent is reluctant to retire, however. If communication between father and son is poor, the mother serves as peacemaker. Often, the son who gets along best with his father is most likely to inherit the farm (Kohl, 1976).

Although legal contracts may define division of labor, lines of authority, and assignment of farm income, thereby decreasing conflict, such contracts may paradoxically increase conflict in that they reduce free-flowing communication between people who assume the contracts are all-inclusive. A feeling of indebtedness to parents can be stressful to the person who inherits or buys the family farm (Bratton & Berkowitz, 1976). In addition, a son losing the family farm may experience an array of emotions from guilt to depression so deep that he contemplates suicide.

There is no consistent pattern of sharing the farm among siblings following the death of the parents. Sometimes, the farm is divided between the off-spring, or one person decides to buy a share of the farm from other family members. If a farm is divided into several smaller portions, the farmer frequently must rent additional land to make farming financially feasible. One son (or daughter) may actually manage the farm, sharing income with siblings who have become absentee owners. Finally, farm children may "marry into" another farm, seek employment in a nearby town, or go to college and move further away from their original locale.

COMMUNICATION IN FARM FAMILIES

It is generally fair to describe the communication patterns of farm families as patriarchal, implicit, authoritative, and traditional. A study on multigenerational farm families indicated that the senior generation perceived a greater family satisfaction, esteem, and communication than did the junior generation. The latter reported a higher level of stress. Although the junior generation had a modern view of the roles of both husbands and wives, sex role discrepancies remained. Men reported higher levels of personal satisfaction and more involvement in decision making, while women reported greater amounts of stress and practiced more coping techniques. The perception of power in decision making fell along sex lines (Blundell, 1985).

In the past, many farm families felt no need for long-range planning in such areas as changes in techniques, job divisions, and estate planning. Thus, those who have dealt with both personal and business matters on a day-to-day basis, find themselves ill-equipped to communicate basic operational changes and potential stressors. Thus, many farm families, particularly those with inter-generational operations, find themselves facing economic hardships and high levels of stress in the 1980s with few tools to assist them in considering such fundamental issues as

- authority and power

    - Who is the boss?
    - Is the younger generation more than hired hands?

- legal issues

    - Are legal arrangements necessary?
    - Are those decisions discussed?
    - Who is involved in the decision-making process?

- family relations

    - Where do loyalties lie—with spouse or parents?
    - How can family conflicts be separated from business issues?

- decision making

    - Who makes the final decisions?
    - Which farm labors are included in farm policy?

In farm families, there is an implicit division of tasks according to both role and gender. In interviews with men in two-generation farm families, the men described decision making as their responsibility, particularly in regard to the farm operation. One man stated, "Mom says I *tell* everyone what to do." The men consistently denied stress (e.g., "Things don't bother me too much."). Many sons added, "As long as things are done as they always have been, it's OK."

The men in both generations viewed their wives as responsible for family maintenance. When asked to list their goals in order of importance, most stated a desire to "pass the farm to the next generation." The younger men, however, frequently mentioned their financial concerns:

Father: We want to pass the farm to the next generation.
Son: My first goal is to get our place paid for.

The fathers reported feeling that they fit "excellently" into the farm operation, while the sons made such statements as "We have sort of an unspoken
partnership." Both reported that stress management was not a problem,
because they "don't let it bother me" . . . "make the best of it" . . . "Dad is sort
of like me." Clearly, those who work with and/or provide services to farmers
must emphasize clarity in communication and specific information.

Young farm women felt that there were some communication problems in
their families:

- "I'd like to have more input on decision making."
- "Dad is not aware that he bothers me as he does."
- "Always having to answer to someone else is a problem."

These statements were often followed by comments such as "I do feel we can
work these things out by sitting down and talking about them." These
communication problems on the farm are magnified in interactions outside the
rural community where perceptions and experiences are different.

HEALTH ISSUES

Farming had the dubious honor of being ranked as the most hazardous
occupation in 1984, above mining and construction. There were 1,600 agricultural work deaths and 160,000 injuries in 1984. Children aged 5 to 14 and
men over 65 have the highest injury rates of all groups on the farm (National
Safety Council, 1985–1986).

Farmers are not paid when they are sick or injured, so they may continue to
work when ill or return to work too soon after an illness or injury (Bubloz &
Eichorn, 1964). Furthermore, like other self-employed people, farmers must
purchase health insurance at individual rates, which tend to be much higher
than health insurance purchased at group rates. The poorer the farmer, the less
likely he is to carry health insurance, thus leaving the family vulnerable to
adverse financial consequences from unforeseen illnesses (Jensen, 1983).

There are other health issues related to poverty. In 1983, 24% of farm
residents had incomes below the poverty level, compared to 15% of nonfarm
residents (De Are & Kalbacher, 1985). Although no research has been done
on the comparative effects of government assistance programs (e.g., school
lunches, food stamps, Medicare, Medicaid) for the farm and nonfarm poor,
anecdotal reports suggest that the gas and travel time expended in obtaining

food stamps often outweigh the benefits for farm families. In addition, farm families may have too many assets on paper to be eligible for food stamps. For example, if the farm family owns two vehicles worth more than $4,500, the family is ineligible for food stamps. Finally, farmers appear to be less likely to sign up for programs that they consider welfare. Most of those who have signed up for welfare during the recent farm crisis have done so only when there was no alternative.

Farm women visit their physicians less often and receive prenatal care later than do nonfarm women. Infant mortality rates, commonly used as standards for health care, are higher in rural settings. Fewer physicians and medical services are available in rural settings where chronic and occupational diseases are prevalent (Bigbee, 1984). One study showed that those physicians now in small towns may not be able to stay because of low collection rates. Elderly farm widows may find it difficult to obtain health care services because of transportation problems and isolation (Kivett, 1978).

The farm crisis has exacerbated the preexisting problems of farm families, creating new barriers to their mental and physical well-being. Although there are few clinical data on this subject, there is anecdotal evidence of an increase in suicides and fatal "farm accidents" among farmers. Crisis and medical clinics are reporting an increased incidence in anxiety disorders, depression, and other affective disorders. Traditionally stable farm marriages are falling apart under the strain of financial ruin, while alcohol abuse and spouse abuse are becoming more common (Heffernan & Heffernan, 1985; Krieger, 1985). Other stress-related illnesses (e.g., peptic ulcer disease) may also be increasing in frequency but no studies have been designed to examine these health effects of the farm crisis.

CONCLUSION

The farm crisis of the 1980s has no end in sight, and many more families will go through the stress of losing the family farm before the present situation has been resolved. The financial stress that a family may experience or the grief that the family shares with friends who have lost their farms will alter, strain, or accentuate familiar patterns of interaction. These families need support and counseling from trained experts, such as physicians, counselors, and social workers. These experts must approach farm families sensitively, as they are often reluctant to seek professional help. Professionals must understand the true importance that the family farm has held in the lives of the family members.

REFERENCES

Beers, H.W. (1935). *Measurements of family relationships in farm families of central New York* (Memoir 183). New York: Cornell University, Agricultural Experiment Station.

Bharadwaj, L., & Wilkening, E.A. (1974). Occupation satisfaction of farm husbands and wives. *Human Relations, 26,* 739–753.

Bigbee, J.L. (1984). The changing role of rural women: Nursing and health implications. *Health Care for Women International, 5,* 307–322.

Blundell, J. (June 1985). Paper presented at a Rural Crisis Workshop for the Iowa Department of Mental Health and Retardation.

Bratton, C.A., & Berkowitz, A.D. (1976). Intergenerational transfers of the farm business. *Food and Life Sciences Quarterly, 9*(2), 7–9.

Bubloz, M.J., & Eichorn, R.L. (1964). How farm families cope with heart disease: A study of problems and resources. *Journal of Marriage and the Family, 26,* 166–173.

Coward, R.T. & Smith, W.M., Jr. (Eds.). (1981). *The family in rural society.* Boulder, CO: Westview Press, pp. 130–139.

De Are, D. & Kalbacher, J. (December 1985). *Farm population of the United States: 1984.* Farm Population Series P-27, No. 58. Washington, DC: U.S. Department of Agriculture.

Dorner, P., & Marquardt, M. (1978, September). *Land transfers and funds needed to start farming: A sample of Wisconsin farms 1950–1975* (Agricultural Economics Staff Paper Series, No. 148). Madison, WI: University of Wisconsin.

Dorner, P., & Marquardt, M. (1979). *The family's role in the Wisconsin family farm* (Agricultural Economics Staff Paper Series, No. 171). Madison, WI: University of Wisconsin.

Fuson, K. (1986, April 19). Farming communities find future of rural life lies outside the fields. *Des Moines Register,* pp. 1, 2A.

Hedlund, D., & Berkowitz, A. (1979). The incidence of social-psychological stress in farm families. *International Journal of Sociology of the Family, 9,* 233–243.

Heffernan, J.B., & Heffernan, W.P. (1985, May). *The effects of the agricultural crisis on the health and lives of farm families.* Paper presented to the Committee on Agriculture, United States House of Representatives. Washington, DC.

Hines, F.K., Green, B.L., & Petrulis, M.F. (1985, December). *Regional impact of financial stress in farming.* Paper presented at the Annual Agricultural Outlook Conference USDA, Washington, DC.

Iowa Farm Bureau Federation, Communications Division. (1985). *Facts on Iowa Agriculture.* Des Moines: Author.

Jensen, H. (December 1983). *Farm people's health insurance coverage.* Rural Development Research Report No. 39. Washington, DC: U.S. Department of Agriculture.

Kada, R. (1978). *Off-farm employment and farm adjustments: Microeconomic study of the part-time farm family in the United States and Japan.* Unpublished doctoral dissertation, University of Wisconsin, Madison, WI.

Kivett, V.R. (1978). Loneliness and the rural widow. *Family Coordinator, 27,* 389–394.

Kohl, S.B. (1976). *Working together: Women and family in southwestern Saskatchewan.* Toronto: Holt, Rinehart & Winston of Canada.

Krieger, L. (1985, October 18). Farmers' health jeopardized by stress. *American Medical News,* pp. 3, 33, 34.

Muhm, D. (1986, January 19). Land prices due for recovery after decline. *Des Moines Sunday Register*, pg. 2X.

National Safety Council. (1985-1986). *Farm Safety Review, 42*(4), 7–10.

Report on Lifestyles/Personal Health Care in Different Occupations. (1979). Kansas City, MO: Research & Forecasts, subsidiary of Ruder & Fine, Inc.

Rosenblatt, P.C., & Anderson, R.M. (1981). In R.T. Coward & W.M. Smith, Jr. (Eds.), *The family in rural society* (pp. 156–159). Boulder, CO: Westview Press.

Singleton, R.S. (1986, April 4). Women break new ground. *Iowa City Press Citizen*, pp. 7, 8A.

Singleton, R.S. (1986, April 7). Farm women change faces. *Iowa City Press Citizen*, pp. 7, 9A.

Stephens, W.N. (1979). *Our children should be working.* Springfield, IL: Charles C Thomas.

Wilkening, E.A., & Ahrens, N. (1979). *Farm work and business roles as related to farm and family characteristics.* Paper presented at Annual Meetings of the Rural Sociological Society, Burlington, VT.

8. The Stress of Unemployment: Its Effects on the Family

Colette Fleuridas, MA, PhD
Community Counseling Center
Salt Lake City, Utah

U nemployment and its effects on the family have been examined in numerous studies that focused on times of economic depression, such as the 1930s, and times of economic recession, such as the 1970s and early 1980s. Although the findings of these studies are varied, there is substantial evidence that undesired joblessness contributes to individual and family stress.

By mid-1986, the civilian unemployment rate in the United States reached 7.3%; nearly 8.6 million U.S. citizens were out of work (U.S. Department of Labor, Bureau of Labor Statistics). This statistic does not include the millions who are underemployed, have only part-time employment, or have become so discouraged that they have simply given up actively looking for work. There are no national statistics on the percentage of unemployed who receive mental health services, nor is it known what percentage of those seeking such services are jobless (R. Manderscheid, personal communication, 1986). It is known that, in Salt Lake County, Utah, approximately 35% of the adults who enter community mental health outpatient units are unemployed (Olsen, 1983). Only recently, however, has the relationship between unemployment and psychological ill health begun to be examined.

The aim of this chapter is two-fold. First, the stressors and the effects of involuntary joblessness on the family will be reviewed. Second, an ecological approach to the treatment of the unemployed family is proposed. The intent is to encourage those in the helping professions to re-evaluate their own conceptualization of the needs and treatment of the jobless, as well as to motivate therapists to assume their role as social advocates of the people they serve.

STRESSORS OF INVOLUNTARY JOBLESSNESS

One of the most stressful of life events is involuntary joblessness (Brenner, 1979; Buss & Redburn, 1983; Cramer & Keitel, 1984; Fagin & Little, 1984). The newly unemployed worker experiences psychological stress as a result of changes in five critical areas (see Fagin & Little, 1984; Jahoda, 1982):

1. daily structure (time, place) and obligatory activity
2. shared experiences and social interaction
3. economics (personal power and autonomy, current financial commitments, and future plans)
4. status, identity, and purpose (present and future)
5. opportunities to develop skills, creativity, and productivity

These changes are typically unwelcome. No longer does an externally enforced structure delimit the person's daily schedule, activities, and predominant social exchange. Most individuals who have been unemployed for some time spend much of their day doing little that they themselves value. Financial hardships may force them and those whom they support to adopt a survival stance. Resources and opportunities to develop new skills or to explore alternatives are limited (Buss & Redburn, 1983; Fagin & Little, 1984).

There are numerous factors that increase an individual's vulnerability to the stress of involuntary joblessness. Prolonged unemployment and financial deficits are the two situational variables most highly correlated with stress (Buss & Redburn, 1983; Fagin & Little, 1984; Moen, 1983). Individuals at special risk for long-term unemployment are those who have few economic, social, and personal resources, such as single heads of households with young children (particularly women); members of minority groups; and unskilled, low-income workers (Moen, 1983; Targ, 1983). Those in geographical areas where there is an economic crisis, as well as middle-aged and older people who find it more difficult to retrain and start over than do younger individuals, are also at risk for prolonged joblessness (Buss & Redburn, 1983; Moen, 1983; Payne, Warr, & Hartley, 1984; Warr & Jackson, 1985).

Traditionally, Western societies blame the unemployed for their unemployment. Ironically, it appears that those who most desire work are the ones who suffer most when they are unemployed for a prolonged period of time. The interaction or accumulation of several stressors, specifically, the desire for a job, increased financial deficits, and length of unemployment, are highly related to psychophysical ill health (Fagin & Little, 1984; Jackson & Warr, 1984; Jahoda, 1982; Komarovsky, 1940; Liem & Rayman, 1982).

The stressors of unemployment on the family parallel those on the individual. The decrease in family resources often leads to inadequacies in the family diet, postponement of all but emergency health care, and limited opportunities for recreational activities. Threats to economic security may necessitate relocation and an adjustment to new neighborhoods, new schools, and new social contacts (Berry & Chiappelli, 1985; Fagin & Little, 1984).

Usually, family members experience changes in their roles and in the amount of time that they spend together. The unemployed partner may spend more time at home, which has numerous ramifications for the couple and parent-child relationships. If one spouse is unable to find work, the other may attempt to find work or to increase the number of hours worked at a job already held. Although the unemployment of women has received less attention than that of men, the financial difficulties caused by the loss of the wife's job are just as great as those caused by the loss of the husband's job in families dependent on both spouses' income (Perrucci, cited in Kleiman, 1986).

Jobless single heads of households face multiple stressors, including their need for adequate and affordable child care. Women who are the sole support of their family make up a larger percentage of the unemployed than of the labor force (Klein, 1983); hence, the feminization of poverty.

In their study of unemployed families, however, Fagin & Little (1984) found that unemployment insurance is inadequate for most families. They felt that the jobless were being punished in this way, even though most of them would rather work than rely on financial aid. Many jobless workers interpret the low level of unemployment insurance as a national statement of their worthlessness. This perception diminishes their self-esteem, their confidence in their present ability, and their willingness to be productive, and they may become more dependent in the long run.

RESPONSE TO THE STRESSORS OF JOBLESSNESS

Few longitudinal studies have been conducted to differentiate the predisposing factors from the consequences of involuntary unemployment. Some longitudinal research has shown that employment status is unrelated to mental health (Catalano & Dooley, 1979; Kasl & Cobb, 1982; Warr & Jackson, 1985); however, most reports indicate that unemployment results in low self-esteem, depressive affect, and increased anger or hostility (Banks & Jackson, 1982; Hayes & Nutman, 1981; Liem & Rayman, 1982; McPherson & Hall, 1983; Stokes & Cochrane, 1984; Winefield & Tiggeman, 1985). Increases in crime; in drug, alcohol, and cigarette use; and in psychosomatic complaints have also been highly correlated with unemployment (Buss & Redburn, 1983; Fagin & Little, 1984; McCormac & Filante, 1984; Pryor & Ward, 1985; Sommer & Lasry, 1984). Recently, Platt and Kreitman (1985) found evidence to support the disputed hypothesis of Brenner (1979) that suicide and parasuicide (i.e., nonfatal, deliberate self-harm) rates increase with long-term unemployment.

There is no universal response to unemployment. Fortin (1984) suggested that the transitional sequence of experiences from job loss to adaptation is similar to that identified in those who must learn to accept a permanent loss (i.e., shock/denial, expectation/hope, anxiety, distress, discouragement, and resignation). These stages of loss have yet to be documented as a predictable pattern after job loss, however (Kasl & Cobb, 1982; Stokes & Cochrane, 1984).

Effects of Unemployment on the Family

The unemployed have an increased incidence of family problems, including marital conflict, child abuse, and spouse abuse (Berry & Chiappelli, 1985; Fagin & Little, 1984; Komarovsky, 1940; Liem & Rayman, 1982; Steinberg, Catalano, & Dooley, 1981). Buss and Redburn (1983) reported that spouses of unemployed workers claim to have more feelings of aggressiveness, helplessness, and victimization. Spouses have also reported an increase in depression, anxiety, and interpersonal conflicts with prolonged joblessness (Liem & Rayman, 1982).

Children, especially those in working class unemployed families, report having more family problems and feeling less mobile, more helpless, and more victimized than do children of unemployed white collar or employed families (Buss & Redburn, 1983; Fagin & Little, 1984; Komarovsky, 1940). Some parents note an increase in behavioral disorders in their children (Fagin & Little, 1984). Many of the problems of children in unemployed families are similar to the problems of children in low-income families, such as a lack of scholastic progress and an increase in somatic complaints (Madge, 1983). Most qualitative research suggests that unemployment does have negative effects on children in that it leads to a decrease in social status, material deprivation, and abuse. There is little definitive evidence to support these claims, however (Madge, 1983).

The loss of a job is apt to interrupt the family's stage of development (Carter & McGoldrick, 1980). Adolescents who were preparing to leave home may need to stay for economic reasons, or they may choose to leave home earlier than planned in order not to burden the family or to avoid conflict (Fagin & Little, 1984).

Occasionally, the unemployed and their spouses describe their family relationships as improved or strengthened by the loss of a job (Fagin & Little, 1984; Thomas, McCabe, & Berry, 1980). A few wives claim to feel better physically since their husband's job loss; this may be the result of increased (enjoyable) time spent together as a family or of the wife's opportunity to seek and accept a job (Fagin & Little, 1984).

Effects of Unemployment on the Community

That massive unemployment affects a community is unquestioned. The long-term societal effects of unemployment have yet to be systematically assessed, however. Shelton (1985) included in the social costs of unemployment not only the lost productivity of the unemployed individual, but also the expenses of providing the services needed to deal with the economic and psychological problems that stem from long-term unemployment. She estimated that the costs of lost productivity, unemployment benefits, and other financial assistance reach $34 billion per year at the recent high unemployment rates.

It is apparent that effects of unemployment are moderated by numerous variables. Knowledge of environmental and personal characteristics that lessen the negative responses to undesired joblessness facilitates the generation of prevention and intervention strategies.

Mitigating Factors

Social support in the form of unemployment benefits, low-cost necessities (e.g., food, clothes, insurance, medical and dental care), part-time work, retraining, and job placement are important moderators of the stress of joblessness (Fagin & Little, 1984; Hayes & Nutman, 1981; Kasl & Cobb, 1982; Kilpatrick & Trew, 1985).

Personal factors (e.g., ability, aptitude, personal resources, and family support) and environmental conditions may mitigate the stress of unemployment. This may be explained best in terms of a transactional stress model (Cameron & Meichenbaum, 1982) in which stress is depicted as a phenomenon that results when (perceived) demands exceed (perceived) resources of the system (Lazarus & Cohen, 1977). Thus, the vulnerability of workers to the stress of unemployment is a function of their appraisal of their needs, the demands of the environment, and their resources to meet these needs and demands. The unique interaction of these variables for each family explains the variability of the effects of unemployment (Lewis, 1986; McCubbin, 1979; McCubbin et al., 1980).

The way in which an unemployed individual evaluates the situation (i.e., demands and resources) is influenced by the appraisal and response of family members and of the larger social context. Even in recessionary times, as Pryor and Ward (1985) demonstrated, there is a tendency for families and society to criticize the individual unjustly. Furthermore, offered support is often inadequate to meet the needs and demands.

The presence or absence of a relational system that provides adequate psychological, social, and material support appears to be the critical factor in an individual's appraisal of and response to involuntary joblessness. Whether negative responses are a function of stress or of the perception that demands exceed resources has yet to be empirically substantiated (Golden & Dohrenwend, 1981). There is, however, ample evidence to indicate that individual and family dysfunction is more likely to occur in the face of criticism, either overt or subtle, and inadequate economic and social resources.

COPING STRATEGIES

McCubbin and associates (1980) described family coping strategies as the process whereby a family achieves and maintains a balance of internal and external conditions that promotes system organization and unity, as well as member independence, self-esteem, and development. Using a cognitive coping process, the family assesses an event in a way that does not disrupt the system. Positive connotations of the event or of other possibilities lead the family together to explore options optimistically. Behavioral coping strategies include a range of actions that decrease the risk of disequilibrium. For example, family members may work together, offering services to the neighborhood (e.g., child care or yard work) to diminish the economic burdens.

Not all coping mechanisms serve their purpose. In order to conserve resources, for example, the unemployed family may delay health care. Family members may increase their use of alcohol and drugs in an effort to cope with the new situation. Children may find seemingly deviant means to distract their parents from their mounting economic and/or marital troubles. These types of coping behaviors typically increase stress and instability in the family.

Coping strategies are attempts to tolerate or even to benefit from a given situation. They include active behaviors intended to influence the environment and to change social and personal circumstances (Pearlin & Schooler, 1978). Many researchers who have studied the effects of unemployment and the outcomes of various interventions have concluded that the most beneficial (coping) response is to seek and find satisfactory reemployment (Fagin & Little, 1984; Fortin, 1984; Pryor & Ward, 1985).

UNEMPLOYMENT INTERVENTION

To the extent that personal, familial, and/or societal factors prevent reemployment, intervention should be directed toward changing these factors.

An additional option is to redefine work and to cultivate other means of obtaining self-worth, identity, activity, social contacts, and financial resources.

Traditional Approach

Traditional models of career and vocational counseling give little attention to the influence and needs of the family, much less to the economic conditions of the nation (e.g., Holland, 1959). Instead, they focus on the individual's needs, interests, abilities, resources, stage of life, and career development, evaluating them and matching them with a corresponding vocation. Unemployment is typically viewed as the responsibility of the individual (Shifron, Dye, & Shifron, 1983).

Family Therapy Approach

Recently, authorities on counseling the unemployed have demonstrated a greater sensitivity to the socioeconomic limits placed on the jobless (Pryor & Ward, 1985), including the family in the therapeutic assessment and treatment of the jobless (Cramer & Keitel, 1984; Herr & Lear, 1984; Luckey, 1974; Shifron et al., 1983; Waldman, 1983; Zingaro, 1983). Recommended therapeutic interventions range from a structural approach to the family (Minuchin, 1974) to group counseling for the children (Berry & Chiappelli, 1985) and communication skill building for the parents (Cramer & Keitel, 1984; Jones, Pearsall, & Gibson, 1984).

Little has been written on the implementation of specific family therapy models in the treatment of the unemployed; researchers have not documented the most beneficial ways to intervene with the unemployed family. Traditional psychotherapy has been found to be of limited value in meeting the needs of the jobless, however (Abbott, 1984; Fortin, 1984). Family therapy in and of itself is also likely to be insufficient when the problem of unemployment is ultimately political and economic (Pryor & Ward, 1985).

Ecological Approach

Comprehensive intervention is designed to address unemployment systemically or ecologically. Critics have recently challenged family systems theorists to reconsider the boundaries of their therapy models and to treat individuals not only within their familial contexts, but also within their community and sociopolitical contexts (James & McIntyre, 1983; Kliman & Trimble, 1983; Liddle, 1985). This approach is particularly appropriate for families that have multiple problems or are socially and economically disadvantaged (Kaplan, 1986; Umbarger, 1972). The ecological approach, however, is recommended for all social classes (Mannino & Shore, 1972).

An ecological investigation consists of a comprehensive evaluation of the unemployed individual's past and present familial, cultural, and social environment. In addition to the belief systems and interactional patterns of the unemployed family, societal values and economic conditions are weighed. Like the family systems approach, the ecological approach relieves the individual of sole blame; furthermore, it enables the family members to see themselves and the joblessness in a social context. They not only look within and among themselves for change, but also are more apt to consider social networks, community resources, and political involvement as a means to meet their needs.

An ecological investigation prompts a comprehensive attempt to effect change at all relevant levels of interaction. Although intervention is directed primarily toward the fulfillment of individual and familial needs, it includes an examination of the social conditions that perpetuate individual and family dysfunction. Thus, the therapist provides the family with the psychological, interpersonal, and career counseling needed (Pryor & Ward, 1985) and with information regarding the economic and political conditions and structural trends that influence employment conditions. The therapist helps family members to conceptualize and utilize their social networks, informing them about community and federal resources (Ashinger, 1985; Biegel, McCardle, & Mendelson, 1985; Cramer & Keitel, 1984; Erickson, 1984; Gottlieb, 1983; Kliman & Trimble, 1983; Leipman, Wolper, & Vazquez, 1982).

If family members express an interest, the therapist can direct them to social advocacy groups and encourage them to spend some of their recently acquired free time constructively involved in learning more about their sociopolitical situation. Many families do not have the interest or the self-confidence to become involved in community affairs. Educating family members about their rights and roles as citizens provides more options for action, however.

Finally, it has been proposed that therapists redefine work and joblessness in a way that lessens the negative effects of the stress of unemployment (Hayes & Nutman, 1981). Alternative concepts of worthwhile employment and additional means of developing a social identity are an integral part of this solution (Webster, 1984).

It has become apparent in the last decade that traditional approaches to vocational counseling and job training are not adequate nor effective forms of unemployment prevention and intervention (Abbott, 1984; Fagin & Little, 1984). An ecological assessment and intervention model has been proposed as the means to address the multiple needs of the unemployed family.

One role of the mental health care provider is to be an advocate of the disadvantaged, impressing those in authority with clients' circumstances and becoming an agent of social change (Adams, 1973; Halleck, 1971). This may be done actively or by providing support to those who choose to give their time and resources to work toward eradicating the conditions that threaten the well-being of the disadvantaged (Atkinson, 1980; Fagin & Little, 1984; Hayes & Nutman, 1981; Jahoda, 1982; Kaplan, 1986; Sunley, 1980; Webster, 1984). Therapists clearly have a vital part in developing, evaluating, and establishing an ecosystemic approach to the primary, secondary, and tertiary prevention of unemployment that will limit the negative effects of preexisting joblessness and will drastically increase the opportunities for a satisfactory life and career for the individual, the family, and the society at large.

REFERENCES

Abbott, M. (1984). Unemployment responses from a community mental health perspective. *Mental Health in Australia, 12,* 24–31.

Adams, H.J. (1973). The progressive heritage of guidance: A view from the left. *Personnel and Guidance Journal, 51,* 531–538.

Ashinger, P. (1985). Using social networks in counseling. *Journal of Counseling and Human Development, 63,* 519–521.

Atkinson, D.R. (1980). The elderly, oppression, and social-change counseling. *Counseling and Values, 24,* 74–85.

Banks, M.H., & Jackson, P.R. (1982). Unemployment and risk of minor psychiatric disorder in young people: Cross-sectional and longitudinal evidence. *Psychological Medicine, 12,* 789–798.

Berry, G.L., & Chiappelli, F. (1985). The state of the economy and the psychosocial development of the school-age child. *Elementary School Guidance and Counseling, 19,* 300–306.

Biegel, D.E., McCardle, E., & Mendelson, S. (1985). *Social networks and mental health: An annotated bibliography.* Beverly Hills, CA: Sage Press.

Brenner, M.H. (1979). Influence of the social environment on psychopathology: The historic perspective. In J.E. Barrett (Ed.), *Stress and mental disorder.* New York: Raven Press.

Buss, T.F., & Redburn, F.S. (1983). *Mass unemployment.* Beverly Hills, CA: Sage Press.

Cameron, R., & Meichenbaum, D. (1982). The nature of effective coping and the treatment of stress related problems: A cognitive-behavioral perspective. In L. Goldberger & S. Breznitz (Eds.), *Handbook of stress: Theoretical and clinical aspects.* New York: The Free Press.

Carter, E.A., & McGoldrick, M. (Eds.). (1980). *The family life cycle.* New York: Gardner Press.

Catalano, R., & Dooley, D. (1979). Does economic change provoke or uncover behavioral disorder? A preliminary test. In L. Ferman & J. Gordus (Eds.), *Mental health and the economy.* Kalamazoo, MI: Upjohn Institute.

Cramer, S.T., & Keitel, M.A. (1984). Family effects of dislocation, unemployment, and discouragement. *Family Therapy Collections, 10,* 81–93.

Erickson, G.D. (1984). A framework and themes for social network interventions. *Family Process, 23,* 187–197.

Fagin, L., & Little, M. (1984). *The forsaken families: The effects of unemployment on family life.* Middlesex, England: Penguin Books.

Fortin, D. (1984). Unemployment as an emotional experience: The process and the mediating factors. *Canada's Mental Health, 32,* 6–9.

Golden, R.R., & Dohrenwend, B.S. (1981). A path analytic method for testing causal hypotheses about the life stress process. In B.S. Dohrenwend & B.P. Dohrenwend (Eds.), *Stressful life events and their contexts*. New York: Prodist.

Gottlieb, B.H. (1983). *Social support strategies: Guidelines for mental health practices*. Beverly Hills, CA: Sage Press.

Halleck, S.L. (1971). Therapy is the handmaiden of the status quo. *Psychology Today, 4,* 30, 32, 34, 98, 100.

Hayes, J., & Nutman, P. (1981). *Understanding the unemployed: The psychological effects of unemployment*. New York: Tavistock.

Herr, E.L., & Lear, P.B. (1984). The family as an influence on career development. *Family Therapy Collections, 10,* 1–15.

Holland, J.L. (1959). A theory of vocational choice. *Journal of Counseling Psychology, 6,* 35–43.

Jackson, P.R., & Warr, P.B. (1984). Unemployment and psychological ill-health: The moderating role of duration and age. *Psychological Medicine, 14,* 605–614.

Jahoda, M. (1982). *Employment & unemployment: A social-psychological analysis*. Cambridge, England: Cambridge University Press.

James, K., & McIntyre, D. (1983). The reproduction of families: The social role of family. *Journal of Marriage and Family Therapy, 9,* 119–129.

Jones, A., Pearsall, P., & Gibson, D. (1984). Unemployed couples' information and discussion groups. *Mental Health in Australia, 1,* 45–54.

Kaplan, L. (1986). *Working with multiproblem families*. Lexington, MA: Lexington Books.

Kasl, S.V., & Cobb, S. (1982). Variability of stress effects among men experiencing job loss. In L. Goldberger & S. Breznitz (Eds.), *Handbook of stress: Theoretical and clinical aspects*. New York: The Free Press.

Kilpatrick, R., & Trew, K. (1985). Life-styles and psychological well-being among unemployed men in Northern Ireland. *Journal of Occupational Psychology, 58,* 207–216.

Kleiman, C. (1986, June 22). Unemployment studies missed boat on women. *The Salt Lake Tribune*, p. 12.

Klein, L. (1983, December). Trends in employment and unemployment in families. *Monthly Labor Review,* 21–25.

Kliman, J., & Trimble, D.W. (1983). Network therapy. In B. Woman & G. Stricker (Eds.), *Handbook of family and marital therapy*. New York: Plenum Press.

Komarovsky, M. (1940). *The unemployed man and his family*. New York: Dryden Press.

Lazarus, R.S., & Cohen, J.B. (1977). Environmental stress. In I. Altman & J.F. Wohlwill (Eds.), *Human behavior and environment* (Vol. 2). New York: Plenum Press.

Leipman, M.R., Wolper, B., & Vazquez, J. (1982). An ecological approach for motivating women to accept treatment for drug dependency. In B.G. Reed, G.M. Beschner, & J. Mondanaro (Eds.), *Treatment services for drug dependent women*. Rockville, MD: NIDA.

Lewis, J.M. (1986). Family structure and stress. *Family Process, 25,* 235–247.

Liddle, H. (1985). Beyond family therapy: Challenging the boundaries, roles, and mission of a field. *Journal of Strategic and Systemic Therapies, 4,* 4–14.

Liem, R., & Rayman, P. (1982). Health and social costs of unemployment. *American Psychologist, 37,* 1116–1123.

Luckey, E.B. (1974). The family: Perspectives on its role in development and choice. In E.L. Herr (Ed.), *Vocational guidance and human development*. Boston: Houghton Mifflin.

Madge, N. (1983). Unemployment and its effects on children. *Journal of Child Psychology and Psychiatry, 24,* 311–319.

Mannino, F.V., & Shore, M.F. (1972). Ecologically oriented family intervention. *Family Process, 11,* 499–505.

McCormac, D.C., & Filante, R.W. (1984). The demand for distilled spirits: An empirical investigation. *Journal of Studies on Alcohol, 45,* 176–178.

McCubbin, H.I. (1979). Integrating coping behavior in family stress theory. *Journal of Marriage and the Family, 41,* 237–244.

McCubbin, H.I., Constance, B.J., Cauble, A.E., Comeau, J.K., Patterson, J.M., & Needle, R.H. (1980). Family stress and coping: A decade review. *Journal of Marriage and the Family, 42,* 855–871.

McPherson, A., & Hall, W. (1983). Psychiatric impairment, physical health and work values among unemployed young men. *Australian and New Zealand Journal of Psychiatry, 17,* 335–340.

Minuchin, S. (1974). *Families and family therapy.* Cambridge, MA: Harvard University Press.

Moen, P. (1983). Unemployment, public policy, and families: Forecast for the 1980's. *Journal of Marriage and the Family, 45,* 751–760.

Olsen, G. (1983). *The demographic report for 1983.* Salt Lake City: Salt Lake County Mental Health.

Payne, R., Warr, P., & Hartley, J. (1984). Social class and psychological ill-health during unemployment. *Sociology of Health and Illness, 6,* 152–174.

Pearlin, L., & Schooler, C. (1978). The structure of coping. *Journal of Health and Social Behavior, 19,* 2–21.

Platt, S., & Kreitman, N. (1985). Parasuicide and unemployment among men in Edinburgh 1968–82. *Psychological Medicine, 15,* 113–123.

Pryor, R.G., & Ward, R.T. (1985). Unemployment: What counselors can do about it. *Journal of Employment Counseling, 22,* 3–17.

Shelton, B.K. (1985). The social and psychological impact of unemployment. *Journal of Employment Counseling, 22,* 18–22.

Shifron, R., Dye, A., & Shifron, G. (1983). Implications for counseling the unemployed in a recessionary economy. *The Personnel and Guidance Journal, 61,* 527–529.

Sommer, D., & Lasry, J. (1984). Personality and reactions to stressful life events. *Canada's Mental Health, 32,* 19–20, 32.

Steinberg, L.D., Catalano, R., & Dooley, D. (1981). Economic antecedents of child abuse and neglect. *Child Development, 52,* 975–985.

Stokes, G., & Cochrane, R. (1984). A study of the psychological effects of redundancy and unemployment. *Journal of Occupational Psychology, 57,* 309–322.

Sunley, R. (1980). Family advocacy: From case to case. In C. Munson (Ed.), *Social work with families.* New York: The Free Press.

Targ, D.B. (1983). Women and the "new unemployment." *Humbolt Journal of Social Relations, 10,* 47–60.

Thomas, L.E., McCabe, E., & Berry, J.E. (1980). Unemployment and family stress: A reassessment. *Family Relations, 29,* 517–524.

Umbarger, C. (1972). The paraprofessional and family therapy. *Family Process, 11,* 147–162.

Waldman, E. (1983, December). Labor force statistics from a family perspective. *Monthly Labor Review,* 16–20.

Warr, P., & Jackson, P. (1985). Factors influencing the psychological impact of prolonged unemployment and reemployment. *Psychological Medicine, 15,* 795–807.

Webster, I. (1984). Health costs of unemployment. *Mental Health in Australia, 1,* 17–23.

Winefield, A.H., & Tiggemann, (1985). Psychological correlates of employment and unemployment: Effects, predisposing factors, and sex differences. *Journal of Occupational Psychology, 58,* 229–242.

Zingaro, J.C. (1983). A family systems approach for the career counselor. *The Personnel and Guidance Journal, 61,* 24–27.

Index

FAMILY THERAPY COLLECTIONS

Volume 1— *Values, Ethics, Legalities and the Family Therapist.* L. L'Abate (Ed.), 1982.

Volume 2— *Therapy with Remarriage Families.* Messinger (Ed.), 1982.

Volume 3— *Clinical Approaches to Family Violence.* L.R. Barnhill (Ed.), 1982.

Volume 4— *Diagnosis and Assessment in Family Therapy.* B.P. Keeney (Ed.), 1982.

Volume 5— *Sexual Issues in Family Therapy.* J.D. Woody and R.H. Woody (Eds.), 1983.

Volume 6— *Cultural Perspectives in Family Therapy.* C.J. Falicov (Ed.), 1983.

Volume 7— *Clinical Implications of the Family Life Cycle.* H.A. Liddle (Ed.), 1983.

Volume 8— *Death and Grief in the Family.* T.T. Frantz (Ed.), 1983.

Volume 9— *Family Therapy with School Related Problems.* B.F. Okun (Ed.), 1984.

Volume 10— *Perspectives on Work and the Family.* S.H. Cramer (Ed.), 1984.

Volume 11— *Families with Handicapped Members.* E. Imber Coppersmith (Ed.), 1984.

Volume 12— *Divorce and Family Mediation.* S.C. Grebe (Ed.), 1984.

Volume 13— *Health Promotion in Family Therapy.* J.R. Springer and R.H. Woody (Eds.), 1985.

Volume 14— *Stages: Patterns of Change Over Time.* D.C. Breunlin (Ed.), 1985.

Volume 15— *Integrating Research and Clinical Practice.* L.L. Andreozzi (Ed.), 1985.

Volume 16— *Women and Family Therapy.* M. Ault-Riché (Ed.), 1985.

Volume 17— *The Interface of Individual and Family Therapy.* S. Sugarman (Ed.), 1986.

Volume 18— *Treating Young Children in Family Therapy.* L. Combrinck-Graham (Ed.), 1986.

Volume 19— *Indirect Approaches in Family Therapy.* S. de Shazer and R. Kral (Eds.), 1986.

Volume 20— *Eating Disorders.* Jill Elka Harkaway (Ed.), 1987.

Volume 21— *Family of Origin Therapy.* Alan J. Hovestadt and Marshall Fine (Eds.), 1987.

Volume 22— *Family Stress.* D. Rosenthal (Ed.), 1987.

FORTHCOMING VOLUMES

Volume 23— *Single Parent Families.* M. Lindblad-Goldberg (Ed.), 1987.

Volume 24— *Systemic Interviewing.* E. Lipchik (Ed.), 1987.

Volume 25— *Counseling Couples.* F. Kaslow (Ed.), 1988.